Earth
Angels

True Stories About Real People

Who Bring Heaven

to Earth

BROADWAY

A hardcover edition of this book was published in 1997 by Broadway Books.

Broadway Books titles may be purchased for business or promotional use or for special sales. For information, please write to: Special Markets Department, Bantam Doubleday Dell Publishing Group, Inc., 1540 Broadway, New York, NY 10036.

BROADWAY BOOKS and its logo, a letter B bisected on the diagonal, are trademarks of Broadway Books, a division of Bantam Doubleday Dell Publishing Group, Inc.

First trade paperback edition published 1998.

Designed by Chris Welch

The Library of Congress has catalogued the hardcover edition as:

Library of Congress Cataloging-in-Publication Data
Biederman, Jerry.
Earth angels : true stories about real people who bring heaven to earth / Jerry and Lorin Biederman.—1st ed.
p. cm.
ISBN 0-7679-0004-9 (hardcover)
1. Altruism—Case studies. 2. Helping behavior—Case studies.
I. Biederman, Lorin, 1964– . II. Title.
BJ1474.B54 1997
177'.7—dc21 97-15365
CIP

ISBN 0-7679-0005-7

98 99 00 01 02 10 9 8 7 6 5 4 3 2

For _____,

my Earth Angel,

_____

_____

_____

_____

_____

_____

_____

To Our Earth Angels

For my mother, Carole Lee Atkinson.
I have watched you as I have grown—your generosity,
your grace, and most of all, your pure and unconditional
love, have been my inspiration. You walk through life giving
people the courage and hope to fulfill their dreams.
Because of you, many of my dreams have been realized.
You are my Earth Angel, and I am so proud that you are my mom.

I love you very much,
Yours, Lorin Michelle

For my mother, Esther Wallace Biederman,
who, as a writer, could just as well have written
this book—and, as a genuine Earth Angel to her
family and all those lucky enough to know her,
could have been written about on every page.

I love you,
Jerry

Contents

Introduction

What are Earth Angels? Whether you know it or not, you've encountered them throughout your life's journey, and you continue to each day.

An Earth Angel can be a teacher who believes in you, or a truck driver who stops to change your flat tire, a hero who runs into a burning building to save a child's life, or someone who simply holds a door open so it doesn't slam in your face. An Earth Angel is the family member whom you've known your whole life, or the stranger who sits next to you on a bus bench for only a few minutes. Every day you are surrounded by Earth Angels—by ordinary people who have earned their wings.

So if you sometimes feel as if you're living in a cold and colorless world, we invite you to take a second look around. Just think, if a natural disaster occurred at this moment and the roof caved in on you, many strangers, regardless of race, creed, gender, or age would come to your rescue. All over the world and in different times throughout history we have seen examples of this—when a human being is in need, it is another human being's instinct to help.

But you don't need a tragedy to find an Earth Angel. If you choose to open your eyes to the goodness in the world, you will see them everywhere!

We invite you to look at your world in a different way, and perhaps reflected in the eyes of your Earth Angels, you'll see colors that you've never seen before.

The spark for this book began four years ago when the two of us met. It was love at first sight. We had never met anyone with exactly the same view of life. Our meeting was like a fairy tale come true and, having found each other, we wanted to live in a fairy tale world.

You know the saying, "When you're in love, the world is in love"? Well, much as we tried to keep on our rose-colored glasses, what we saw forced us to acknowledge that the world was *not* in love (the local news, alone, provided evidence).

We quickly realized that one of our mutual passions, besides writing, was our desire to somehow make the world a better place.

We wanted to find a way to help reverse the direction of modern society and have the pendulum swing back to a more innocent time when neighbors talked with each other and kids played safely in the streets.

Having finally found each other, after such a long search for true love, gave us faith that we could find the world we longed for.

We wondered if changing the world could be as easy as changing the way we look at the world. Could it be as simple as seeing the glass half full rather than half empty?

One day we decided to conduct an experiment. What if we spent an afternoon searching for evidence of human kindness? How difficult would it be to find?

We drove to what is considered a bad part of town. We parked in a residential neighborhood and began walking toward a nearby mall.

First we observed a businessman across the street. He was obviously in a hurry, but we saw him stop and take the time to pet a little dog.

Next we noticed kids in a driveway washing their parents' car. They were spraying each other with water, throwing soap suds, and laughing.

When we arrived at the mall, we were hot from the long

walk. In the food court we spotted an ice cream shop and decided to treat ourselves. While we were looking at the rainbow of mouth-watering flavors, we heard a little voice behind us scream, "Nana, I dropped my ice cream!"

We turned to see a curly-haired girl with an empty cone in her hand. On the ground was a big, pink, melting scoop.

As her bottom lip began to tremble, the teenage boy behind the counter said, "Come here. Here's another one with your name on it."

The grandmother pulled a wrinkled Kleenex out of her sleeve and did her best to clean up the mess, while the little girl, now smiling, reached for the fresh ice cream.

"I pushed it down really good this time," the boy said, as he handed her the new cone.

"You're an angel," the grandmother said to the boy. "Say thank you to the young man, Jenny."

Everywhere we turned, we saw kindness.

On the way back to our car, we noticed a boy who looked like a gang member, with baggy pants, dark sun glasses, and a crew cut. He was sitting on a bus bench next to a woman with a baby. He had taken off his thick gold chain and was dangling it playfully over the baby's face. The baby was giggling and trying to reach for it. All were smiling.

In the car, we talked about how we just as easily could have come away from our afternoon at the mall frustrated because we couldn't find a good parking space, annoyed at being sprayed from a hose by rowdy kids, complaining that the bottoms of our shoes were sticky from who knows what, and feeling threatened by the presence of a gang member.

Instead we realized that when you look for the good you find it all around you, and the bad seems to disappear. What you choose to perceive is what you often get—good *or* bad. So why not look for the good? Our challenge was to find a way to share our experience with the world. We wanted people to see life the way we had seen it on this particular day.

As we drove closer to home, we remembered that the grandmother had called the boy at the ice cream shop an "angel." And suddenly it hit us. We realized that we are all surrounded by angels each and every day. Not just ethereal beings, but "Earth Angels"—human beings who *act* like angels. Unlike angels from heaven, Earth Angels are tangible people with whom we can share a smile or a hug.

Being writers, we decided we would interview people about the Earth Angels in their lives, and so we started collecting stories. When we began our writing journey, we weren't sure if we could find enough material to fill a book. We started by talking to our own family and friends; then checkers at our grocery store, servers in neighborhood restaurants, strangers at the park . . . and soon our world began to fill with color.

Before we knew it, the stories in our filing cabinets overflowed onto our living room floor, and soon our house was piled high with wonderful, heartwarming tributes. What began as a search for Earth Angel stories in our hometown—the City of Angels—had extended across America and parts of the world.

We were overwhelmed!

An entire high school devoted their first annual "Writing Across the Curriculum" to *Earth Angels*. Over two thousand students wrote about a special person in their life who had made a positive difference. Some wrote about their parents, grandparents, sisters, and brothers. Others thanked their friends, teachers, and neighbors. Many wrote about a stranger.

Everyone, no matter who we asked, had an Earth Angel story to share. We met many of the storytellers face-to-face, and our interview usually ended with a hug. Some called us on our twenty-four-hour Earth Angels hotline, and many stories arrived in our post office box already beautifully written.

We learned that some of the storytellers had never had the opportunity to thank their Earth Angel, nor had they thought about who their Earth Angel was—until asked.

And so our little afternoon experiment at the mall became a seed that has grown into this book.

We want you, our reader, to realize more than ever that *your* life is blessed with Earth Angels, and we hope that these stories will inspire you to become an Earth Angel in the lives of others.

You may read this book from cover to cover, thumb through and read at random, or let the book fall open, and wherever it does, you will meet an Earth Angel. Just remember, every story is a gift and we wouldn't want you to leave any unopened.

We promise that you will laugh, shed tears, and—most certainly—be touched by an Earth Angel.

Welcome to a heartwarming and loving place—the land of

Earth Angels. It is not a fantasy world. Actually, it's *your* world. Perhaps you just didn't realize that you've been standing at its open door all along . . .

Who is the Earth Angel in your life?

—*Lorin and Jerry*

It is one of the goals of human beings
to develop to the point where life
is aligned to God in such a way
that we behave like an angel
in complete service to heaven.
  —K. Martin-Kuri (from "The Sacred
  Face of Angels," *Angel Times)*

Chapter 1

The Earth Angel Next Door (Friends and Neighbors)

Dear George:
Remember, no man is a failure who has friends.
Thanks for the wings.
Love, Clarence
—From Frank Capra's, "It's A Wonderful Life"

One morning we were seated in a large booth at a local diner. Excited about our search for Earth Angels, we pushed our breakfast plates aside in order to make room for pen and paper.

We had our notebooks with us and were telling each other stories we had recently heard.

The waitress came over to collect our plates and offer more hot chocolate. When we looked up to say thank you, we saw that her head was tilted and she was looking down at the paper.

1

"I'm sorry, I didn't mean to be nosy," she said, somewhat embarrassed. "It's just that the word ANGELS caught my eye, and I love angels."

We told her it was okay and began to describe our book. The next thing we knew, the waitress, Noreen, was sitting in our booth talking expressively about an Earth Angel who had changed her life.

Half an hour later Noreen walked us all the way out to our car. "I had no idea, when I woke up this morning, that I would tell two perfect strangers such a personal story. It felt good to get it out," she said. "I'm here every Sunday. Please come back and let me know how your search is going. God bless you."

She gave us both a hug, and we watched as this woman, no longer a stranger, walked back into the restaurant.

Noreen was among the first of many people we met who invited us into their lives by sharing their personal stories.

These stories show that we are surrounded every day by people who are close enough to know when we are in need. These people can instantly transform from friend or neighbor into our very own Earth Angel.

Flowers from Our Garden

Noreen • 48 • Waitress

I am in my late forties and have two teenage daughters. My life has been difficult but, by the grace of God, I am a survivor.

My girls and I spent much of their childhood in shelters and living on the street. Though we were together six years, I never married the girls' father. He couldn't hold a job and although I am a hard worker, without a college education, the money just wasn't enough to support us. He spent most of my money on hard liquor, and he didn't come home for days at a time.

One day, after he had threatened to kill me (he was a violent drunk), I packed up my babies and our belongings and headed for a better part of town. I figured I would give my girls a good education, even if we had to live on the street.

I managed to find a job as a waitress at a local coffee shop and I enrolled my girls in a good public school. My job didn't pay enough for rent, so we moved from shelter to shelter. I was nervous about the address, so I got a post office box and used that address for the school paperwork.

No one suspected we were homeless. My girls went to school every day. If the shelter was nearby, we would walk. If we had to, we took a bus.

My girls were always very presentable. I let them go to friends' houses as much as possible, and I often tried to buy them special gifts. But, mostly, the little money we had was put away for their future.

We had made a pact that we would not tell anyone we were homeless because I was sure this fine school wouldn't allow my daughters to remain if they knew about our situation.

One day, several years later, one of the girls came back to the shelter and told me her friend's mother had invited all three of us over for supper the next evening. I managed to talk the director of the shelter into allowing me to use the kitchen to bake cookies.

We knocked on the door of a beautiful two-story home. It was spotless and comfortable. Mary, the mother, was so appreciative of the cookies. We had a wonderful evening and I knew I had found a friend.

A few days later, Leticia, my youngest, came home and said that Mary had asked for our phone number. She wanted to call me to get together. Leticia told her we were having trouble with the phones and she would have *me* call *her*. I hated that my girls had to lie.

I called Mary and again we got together at her house. She and I became good friends. I constantly told her that I wanted to have her over to our place, but then I would lie and say we were having trouble with the landlord of our apartment building or that something wasn't working (the stove, the air conditioning . . .).

Mary came into the coffee shop one day and asked if I could spend my break with her. We took a walk, and then she stopped at a vacant house a few blocks down the road. It had a "For Rent" sign out front and was the most adorable little home.

Mary said, "Do you like this place?"

"Oh, very much!" I exclaimed. "But it's way out of my league."

"Why don't we call and find out?" Mary said.

This was upsetting to me. I told her that the most I could afford was $350 a month. No one would rent a house for that little—especially *this* house.

The next day, Mary came into the coffee shop with a big grin on her face and a "For Rent" sign in her hands. She was so excited that she couldn't hold back the news. "I spoke with the owner of that house and guess what? They're renting the place for $350 a month! It couldn't be more perfect for you and the girls."

I told her, "That's impossible. Houses rent for three times that much in this neighborhood."

She explained that the owners didn't really need the money. They just needed someone who would appreciate living there and would take special care of it.

A few weeks later, we moved in. We managed to get some furniture from the Salvation Army. Shari, my oldest, took wood shop in school and made us a fine coffee table. We fixed the place up, and I even planted some flowers, which made me feel like I was planting my roots. I hoped to stay here a long time, raise my girls, and always have a place for them to come home to.

But secrets, I've found, don't usually stay secrets. One month, I had to mail my rent check, but it was during the holidays and I didn't want it to be late so I decided to drop it off at the appropriate post office box. I was standing in line at the post office when I heard a familiar voice ask for a package from the box where I sent my rent. I peeked around the line and was shocked to see Mary!

She was thumbing through her mail when I touched her arm. Tears were starting to form in my eyes and I could barely speak. "Mary, is it *your* house we're living in? Did you do this for us?"

She put her arm around my shoulder and walked me outside. By the time we reached the sidewalk, I was sobbing. I am a very strong woman and tears don't come easily. I have been through a lot in my life, but no one had ever been so kind.

Mary told me that Leticia had slipped and told her daughter we were homeless. She said she never would have guessed. The girls were always so clean and well-dressed. She said it was her and her husband's first home and it was very special to them, that they had owned the house for a long time, and it was paid for. She and her husband had talked about it and wanted to rent the house to us. She hadn't wanted me to know because she was afraid I would think it was charity.

Shari is graduating from high school this year, and because we were able to save enough money, she is going to college.

Mary is my Earth Angel, and I want her to know that I appreciate her kindness and generosity, and that I love her.

I bring Mary fresh flowers every week from our garden.

My Gardening Angel

Connie Poss • 35 • Physical Therapist

My Earth Angel came to me in the form of an elderly man with soil under his nails, a thickness around the middle, and an even thicker accent.

The first time I met him was in his garden. He was tending his beloved well-kept rows of tomatoes, cucumbers, and assorted vegetables. Along his fence grew thick veins of grapevines, and nearby, scattered throughout the yard, were rose bushes and colorful flower beds. When he spoke, his deep booming voice was thick with a heavy Greek accent.

His name was Theo, or more formally, Theodore Androulidakis, and for a brief time, he was my neighbor.

It was my youngest son, Jeffrey, three at the time, who met Theo first. Having just moved to our new home near the foot of the Wasatch Mountains and having no friends yet, he was drawn to the lush greenery of Theo's backyard. Playing their human version of cat and mouse, my son would hide behind the thick vines and wait until he was spotted by this jovial gardener who would then shout a mock warning. With smiles on both their faces, Jeffrey would run home giggling and the sound of Theo's hearty laughter would ricochet off the houses.

Soon Theo invited Jeffrey into his magical garden. He showed him how to pull weeds and water the deep troughs dug carefully beside each row. "This is how it's done in Greece," he would say, smiling as they worked in unison.

They became nearly inseparable and continued the friendship outside the garden as well. Their bond seemed to pull all of us together. In the warm summer evenings, my husband, both our sons, and I would take our lawn chairs to Theo's driveway where we would enjoy the view and the company of Theo, his wife, Mary, and occasionally one or more of his adult children. Though Matthew, our oldest, was shy, it was obvious that Theo had found a way into his heart, as Matthew would sit quietly next to Theo and listen to him speak.

As the summer harvest neared an end and I watched the cottonwood leaves change from summer green to vibrant shades of red and gold, I realized that more had grown in the garden that year than fruits and vegetables. The true bounty had been friendship.

The tilling of the earth—a gardener's sacrifice to next year's rich soil—was completed and the gardening tools put away, but the bond between my sons and Theo remained. As Theo himself said more than once, he loved them like his own. I suppose it was natural that Jeffrey, the outgoing opposite to his shy older brother, displayed his affection most. It was not unusual for Jeffrey to run across the street, after he was bathed and readied for bed, to kiss Theo goodnight.

Through the winter months Theo introduced my sons to things they had never experienced, like wonderful *dolmades* and *spanakopitta*, Mary's Greek cookies, and even professional wrestling. They got a kick out of hearing him shout at the spandex-clad men, using the same booming voice that had carried to my kitchen window those first few days after our arrival.

He told them about Greece, shared with them his plans for a visit there the next summer, and wiped away the tears of my youngest who was crushed that he couldn't go along.

Retired, Theo seemed to have the luxury of judging the passing of time, not by a watch that measures minutes and hours, but by experiences and special moments. His open arms and willing lap seemed to say that he was in no hurry, that there was plenty of time.

But he was wrong; there was not plenty of time.

It is shocking to see panic etched in the faces of your children and to feel it echo wildly inside your own heart. It's a day and a scene that I will never forget. Nothing could have prepared us for that lazy June day when we rounded the corner in our car to see flashing lights and an ambulance at Theo's curb. . . .

We followed his progress through occasional updates from his family. After he had been in the hospital two days, I remember feeling a sense of urgency, the need to go to the hospital to see him. I had to see this man whose heart was betraying him, a heart that had seemed as strong and steady and warm as any I could ever imagine.

On my way to the hospital, the song "Tears in Heaven" by Eric Clapton came on the radio and I knew that Theo was gone. It was difficult to drive while I listened to lyrics that asked, "Would you know my name, if I saw you in heaven?" I knew the answer was yes, that I would know Theo anywhere and that he would be part of me forever. I just wasn't ready to let him go so soon.

I never realized the impact Theo had had on my life until he was no longer in it. In the weeks following his death, I felt as if he were watching over me, trying to tell me that there was a reason we had been given time together, and that it had indeed been a gift.

The beauty of Theo's garden is that it continues to reap a harvest. Everyone in my family has been touched by his life and death, each in their own private and special way. However fleeting his time with us was, he changed our lives forever. I have come to realize that there were many things that grew in Theo's garden beyond the tomatoes and grapevines, and even beyond the friendship.

For my children, love grew—love of nature, love of the earth, love of their newfound ability to nurture something and watch it grow. But mostly, love for this kind man who opened his heart and life to them and showed them that they were more treasured than any plant he could ever grow.

For my husband, a tear grew—the only one I have ever seen him shed. It showed a softness and tenderness that I knew was there but had rarely glimpsed, and it made me love him even more.

I believe the gift he planted for me was words. In his passing I felt the need to write, so as to make his garden live forever for my sons. If they couldn't toil in the garden with him, perhaps I could paint the image of it with my words so that they might continue to feel the sun upon their backs and the dirt beneath their nails, as if they were still there with Theo.

Sometimes I feel Theo with me when I write—coaxing me to listen to all the words and feelings I have inside, and not just those about him. He is encouraging me to let them out into the sunlight to grow—just like the seeds in his garden.

It has been three years since Theo's death. I still think of him often and I still shed an occasional tear. That I only knew him for a year seems impossible; it feels as if I had known him forever. And I know that if there are angels here on Earth, he was one, and I consider myself very lucky.

A framed picture of Theo and my son Jeffrey sits on a shelf in a hallway I pass through each day. It was taken as they planted the last garden that spring, just weeks before his death. In the picture Theo is turned, looking at me, smiling. I think his eyes are telling me to believe—in love, in my children, in myself, and perhaps even in angels.

If I close my eyes and listen just right, I can still hear his laughter bouncing off the walls and into my heart.

The Day a Fort Was Built

Jeremy Taylor • *14* • *Hobbies: Drawing, Playing the Clarinet*

When I was in the fifth grade I was at my best friend Cory's house helping him build a fort in a partially wooded area by a creek. It was January in Ohio, about twenty-five degrees Fahrenheit, and I needed to ride my bike home to get a warmer pair of gloves.

Cory was worried that I might crash, because the roads were very icy and the ground was covered with snow, but I told him I would be fine, that I'd be careful.

When I got home, my hands were freezing, so I went upstairs to the bathroom to soak them in some warm water. As I was doing that, the phone rang and my grandma picked it up, but I couldn't hear who it was. When I finished I got my gloves and got ready to go. On my way downstairs, my grandma told me that she hadn't known I was home. She told me that Cory had called to make sure I'd made it.

I quickly got on my bike and headed for his house. About halfway there, I saw Cory talking to someone in a car. I waited until he was finished, then asked him who it was.

"I'm not sure," he said. "I was just asking people if they had seen you. When I called your house and your grandma said you weren't there, I got worried."

I thought it was neat that I had a friend who cared so much

about me. This happened about four years ago, but because Cory showed true friendship, he will always be an Earth Angel to me.

A Flock of Angels

Richard Grant • 40 • Director of a Home School Program

By chance, my wife and I had to have surgery at the same time. Neither of our operations could wait; we didn't have a choice. What's more, the operations were going to leave us flat on our backs for at least six weeks. We have two young children and we knew this would be a very difficult time.

While in the hospital, we received a phone call from a woman who was a member of the at-home schooling program my wife and I run. The questions she asked were not normal school questions. Instead, they were personal questions regarding the types of foods my family and I preferred.

The evening my wife and I returned from the hospital, there was a knock at the door. My son answered it. Cathy, the woman who had called, and her husband entered our home carrying pots and Tupperware filled with a complete three-course dinner!

They set the table and said they would be back the next day

to collect the dirty dishes (they stressed the word "dirty" because they didn't want us to do any cleaning). They also said that they had made up a list of people from the school, and each day someone would come by to bring us food.

Sure enough, each day someone new arrived with a meal, and there was always enough for us to have lunch the next day. Some even brought a tablecloth, flowers, and candles. Needless to say, we were overwhelmed.

This continued for nearly three months. It even got to the point where we had to call Cathy and tell her to let everyone know not to bring any more salad dressing, as we had collected enough to last a year.

Finally we were feeling better, and we called everyone to thank them and let them know that we would now be cooking for ourselves.

The following day my wife made a wonderful dinner. When we sat down and began to eat, my son said, "Mmm, this is good. Who brought it?" We all laughed and decided to say grace once again to thank God for sending so many Earth Angels to take care of us in our time of need.

Sister Anna

Trisha • 50 • Dentist

Iimmigrated to the United States from my native country,
Romania, over twenty-one years ago. I left with my husband
and my five-year-old daughter. We settled in Phoenix, Arizona,
where I gave birth to my second daughter. My husband knew a
little English, so he was able to get a job with the Coca Cola
company, while I stayed home with my two daughters and tried
to learn English.

We had left Romania with nothing and had arrived in the
United States with nothing; we were desperately poor. My new-
born daughter's crib was the top drawer of our dresser. Our
spirits were high, though; we loved being in America.

One day while my husband was at work and I was at home
with the children, there was a knock at the door. I opened it to
find a nun standing before me. She smiled and asked if she
could come in. I opened the door wider and pointed to the
couch. She sat down and explained that she was from a church
down the street and had heard about our plight from some
members of the church. With the little English I had learned, I
was able to understand what she was saying.

"Our church wants to help you and your family. We understand your situation and we have resources that can assist you,"
she said, as she touched my hand. She spoke slowly so that I

could understand, then continued, "Our church will provide your family with food and clothes. If you need medical care, we will also provide that. Once a week there will be deliveries of all your necessities. We only ask that you donate a dollar a month for the services and that you use the service only as long as you need it. When your family is better settled in and no longer needs the service, we ask that you discontinue it. Do you understand?"

My eyes began to swell with tears, and I was only able to nod my head.

She got up and headed toward the door. She turned around and said, "The first delivery will be this afternoon. If there is anything else that you need, just give us a call. Here is our number."

I pointed at her and asked, "Name?"

"I'm sorry, I forgot to introduce myself. My name is Sister Anna," she said with a smile.

"Thank you," I said, as I held her hand in mine. I moved closer to her and gave her a hug, whispering thank you over and over again.

My husband was offered a job in Los Angeles, so we left within a year of that initial meeting.

I have never forgotten what Sister Anna did for my family. She helped us in a desperate time and I just want to thank her once more for being our Earth Angel.

Giving Thanks

Michelle Lynn Stoker • *17* • *Goal: Writer*

I guess you could say that I'm like most people who have been given everything they ever wanted. I took it all for granted—the food on our table, the roof over my head, and the clothes in my closet. I had a great life: I made the soccer team, got the position I wanted on the school newspaper, tried out for cheer-leading and made it, and was elected to the student council. Everything I've gone for, I've gotten. Nothing bad had ever really happened to me. That is, until my life took a complete turn for the worse.

In early October we got the terrible news that my dad had gotten laid off from work. He was one of many people who lost their jobs because the company had to cut costs. There had been no warning. In fact, my parents had just bought two new cars. (If God was watching over us, he was taking a long nap when this happened.)

My dad remained very positive and was determined to get a new job right away. He had been working since he was nine years old, and work was a very important part of his life. He wanted, so much, to be able to provide for his family as he always had.

But day after day, my dad was out of work, and though we tried to go on as usual, it was getting more difficult for me, my parents, and my younger sister. Days turned into weeks and weeks into months, and we were falling apart.

As the holidays approached, our situation really hit home. We would hear about people going out to nice meals, shopping for holiday gifts together, and traveling to visit relatives. For the first time in my life, we couldn't do any of these things.

We had become poor—no money in our pockets, and bills left unpaid. Yet I still had to go to school and act as if my life was as perfect as it had been; I kept my pain inside.

On the day before Thanksgiving (it had been almost two months since my dad was laid off), I found myself in English class with tears flowing down my face. I could no longer pretend that everything was okay. All my life, on Thanksgiving, my family had given to the poor, but it would be different this year. This year we were in need of food *ourselves*. But we couldn't swallow our pride and reach out.

I told my friend, Angie Federico, that my family wasn't having a Thanksgiving because we didn't have any food. Angie and I had met in junior high, but we hadn't really become friends until high school when I encouraged her to run for student council. It took a lot for me to be honest and to open up, but I felt that I could trust her.

Later that day, I received a call from her. She said, "I want your family to have the best Thanksgiving ever." She told me that she had just cashed her paycheck and gone out and bought a turkey, potatoes, pie, and other food for my family.

This was such a thoughtful act—a seventeen-year-old using

her own paycheck to help a friend and her friend's family. It wasn't the food, but Angie's kindness, that made her my Earth Angel. I don't know if she realizes it, but before her offer, I was thinking that nothing good would come of this terrible thing that had happened. Through Angie's actions, my family and I were able to see that there was still goodness in our lives. Through this we realized that caring for each other is the most important thing.

It is now two weeks after Thanksgiving. My dad's working situation still hasn't changed. But, thanks to my dear friend Angie, my spirits and those of my family have been lifted, and I've begun to find pleasure in the little things in life.

My mom is working two jobs, and my dad is working on the side while looking for a good job. We have faced the fact that we are going to lose our house and cars, but at least, no matter where we are, my family will be together.

I will never lose touch with Angie. Her act of generosity was what I needed on Thanksgiving. Now I truly know the meaning of *thanks-in-giving*. I hope others who are going through this will see the good in their lives. I also hope that those who aren't struggling appreciate the people in their lives more than they do their possessions.

(I dedicate this story to my family, who is struggling at the present time.)

The Earth Angel and the Cherub

Jennifer Jane Ringler • *16* • *Goal: Veterinarian*

Wings? Don't think so. Halo? Not really. Harp? Hardly. He's not the musical type. But he is lovable, quiet, calm, and always sympathetic.

He's tall and handsome, has long brown wavy hair and the biggest brown eyes you would ever see—you could swim in them.

He's the kind of guy any girl could fall in love with. He's always available when I need a hug, he knows when I'm not happy, and he doesn't give up until he's changed my storm clouds into sunshine. It's hard to believe that someone so young can be so wise and wonderful.

Once, I took him to meet some children at a party some friends were having. There were many active little kids there—all hands, feet, and grins running around on the grass.

At first he was shy and sort of hung back, unsure of asserting himself. I was afraid that the children might be a little overwhelming for him. They bounced and played, and their laughter echoed across the yard. My friend must have sensed that it was okay to join in the fun, and soon he was running and playing with them.

They did all the things little ones like to do until they tumbled, in a pile of puffing, panting smiles. He stayed with them until they calmed down, and he responded happily to their hugs and snuggles—with a warmth uniquely his own.

I stood there watching and shared their joy, remembering my own childhood.

When the children began to wind down a bit, I noticed a small child in a corner of the yard out of reach of the activity. His crystal-clear blue eyes were moist with longing as he watched his friends romp and play. This sad little cherub sat alone on the grass, and I could tell he wished that he could join in the fun. But he was unable to run, for all but his smile was crippled by fate: a disease kept him bound to a wheelchair.

When my friend noticed the little boy, he stopped playing with the other children and walked hesitantly to the corner of the yard.

Is it safe? Can he play? Should I stay?

These unspoken questions, which seemed to linger in the air, were answered by the little boy's small, withered hand. It raised up in greeting, and my friend, instinctively, moved close enough to meet it. He lay down beside the boy, and I could tell that they were communicating without words. My friend seemed to know that though this little cherub could not run, he still needed the presence of a friend to feel loved.

My friend, my dog Camden, is truly an Earth Angel. In June he is going to San Rafael for formal training to become a seeing-eye dog. I will miss him, but I know that someday a blind person will also see him as their Earth Angel.

A Will

Bob Sullivan • 81 • Retired Oil Field Services Operator

"Can you come over next Saturday?" read a note placed in our mail box. "I have a job no one else can do." It was signed, "Harry Farmer."

I was fourteen years old, and I'd received many similiar requests from my neighbor. So, the next Saturday, I rode my bike some four miles to his farm.

Harry not only looked like a recluse, he lived like one too—mainly because most of his neighbors were repulsed by his unkempt appearance, especially the tobacco juice that decorated the front of his shirt and bib overalls. When he went to town every week or two for groceries, however, he looked quite respectable—not dressed up—but like most farmers when they went to town.

During the three or four years we lived the quarter mile from Harry—in a rented house and outbuildings—we pastured our cow at his place, and that was how I got acquainted with him.

So the two-cent postcard request that I do some work for him was not surprising. The job was probably some small task like checking the flood gate at the creek crossing or checking fence lines for missing steeples. It had become obvious that his requests for me to work were a ploy, and that his *real* need was for company. When each task was completed, we would talk about many things.

This time the routine had changed. He asked me to come into the two-room bungalow. Then he had me pull out and open an old trunk. He said, "On the tray there is an envelope addressed to you. Please take it out."

When I opened it, I got the surprise of my life. It contained a will to his sixty-acre farm and buildings addressed to me! He told me he had one brother who lived in the sand hills some two hundred to three hundred miles away, and that he too was a bachelor who owned several hundred acres of hay land he didn't need.

Harry knew of my family's need. Mom was a recent widow with eight children and little source of income. A year after Dad died, one of my two younger siblings died from a ruptured appendix. Very early in life we learned that we each needed to contribute according to our capability.

My mother taught us that we could be anything we wanted, and that we didn't have to stay on the farm, but before Harry's gift, I really had no ambition.

I didn't think that going to his house was anything extraordinary, but it had been friendship that Harry craved. My mother thought it was wonderful that a person would be so generous just for friendship.

Because I received the will and legal papers needed to acquire the farm, I felt a responsibility toward his well-being, as well as a sympathy. So I was in contact with him more often than before.

In January 1935, I joined the CCC (Civilian Conservation Corps) and served in soil conservation projects in southeast Nebraska. In June I got word that Harry was not well, so I promptly left the Corps to take care of him.

Doctors made house calls in those days and so when we arrived we were told that his condition was terminal. Billy, his brother, came too, and we nursed him together for a few weeks until he died. Billy was pleased that I was there and that Harry had willed the farm to me.

Because of Harry's generosity, I no longer lived just to survive. Getting the farm gave me the opportunity to go to college.

Harry was a genteel man and he died peacefully. I remember my friend often in my prayers, which are, possibly, more *to* him than *for* him. Harry was a quiet and kind Earth Angel.

Fast Food from the Heart

Jo-Ann Nipper • *64* • *Restaurant Employee*

When I was young my parents and I ran a small neighbor-hood grocery. We opened our doors in 1953 and they stayed open for close to thirty years. Tom Pierce was one of our customers. Tom had just gotten married again and we were apprehensive about the marriage lasting. When Tom brought his new wife, Hilda, to meet us, we liked her at once. Her warm personality and great sense of humor made us feel comfortable and brightened our day. She had a glow about her that you could almost see.

In 1978 my dad died. For the next three years, my mother and I tried to run the grocery ourselves, until my mom's health began to fail, and we had to sell it. I stayed home for the next eleven years to look after her. We struggled financially, trying to get by on her Social Security and a small, fast-dwindling savings account.

Hilda was one of the few customers who continued to keep in touch. She never forgot us at Christmastime or on birthdays.

When Mom passed away I was left with very little. I also had the disadvantage of being a middle-aged woman with few skills. It was at this time that I discovered how really wonderful Hilda Von Fields Pierce could be. She managed a fast-food restaurant called Mrs. Winners, and, after the funeral service, she brought a generous amount of food to my home. While we were clean-ing in the kitchen, she, knowing my desperate situation, quietly offered me a job at her restaurant.

I was reluctant to take her up on the offer, as I feared I wouldn't be able to do the work and she would have to fire me. That would have hurt her even more than me. I tried to find work elsewhere, but was unsuccessful. Since I was unable to drive, it made matters even worse.

But Hilda knew how to get around my stubborn resistance. She called and told me that she was so short of help she didn't know what she was going to do. I immediately volunteered to come and assist her in any way I could. She happily told me she would pick me up the next morning at seven.

That was four years ago, and I am still there. During this time I have gotten to know my Earth Angel very well. She's been managing Mrs. Winners for over fifteen years (she's only in her mid-forties). Everyone who works for her adores and admires her. She has a tremendous amount of tolerance, patience, sym-pathy, and generosity, and she is a true believer in second chances. Former employees, who left without notice or simply didn't cut it, are often rehired and allowed to try again. She knows about their families and their problems and always has time to listen. She really understands when people have hard-ships. When employees have an illness in their family, she says, "You go right on and be with them." She then calls and inquires after them. All she asks in return is that they do their best on the job. She trains them well—teaching them how to best cook the chicken, use the registers, properly count back change, and, especially, how to make Mrs. Winners' famous biscuits.

We do more business than any other Mrs. Winners franchise in Tennessee, and I'm sure it's because of Hilda. The style of the restaurant is that of a little yellow house with a white picket fence, but to us, it's more than just the style, because Hilda makes it feel like a real home.

She radiates warmth and she loves people. No matter how down you are, she does everything she can to cheer you up. There are around thirty of us working for Hilda and we all say that if she ever leaves, we'll leave with her and follow her anywhere.

Hilda handles her business as well as her large family with ease and grace. After twenty-six years, she and Tom Pierce are still together. Every chance I get, I tell Tom how lucky he is to have her.

Hilda has given me encouragement, friendship, and understanding. She has never failed to be there when I need her. I believe this world would be a lonelier and sadder place without her, and I thank her every day for being my friend.

So the next time you're in Cleveland, Tennessee, stop in for some chicken and dumplings, and a few of our famous biscuits! And you may just find an Earth Angel behind the counter with a name tag that reads, "Hilda."

Wally's Keys

K. S. Nymoen • *40* • *File Clerk and Wedding Coordinator*

K eys were the first thing I noticed about my Earth Angel. He was unlocking a door with one of the dozens of keys he wore on the industrial-strength ring attached to his wide leather belt.

My family and I had come for an appointment with the minister of St. James Lutheran Church. We were very early and the janitor, Wally Krahn, was the only one there to let us in. Deep laugh lines emphasized his smile as he held the door open for us.

Wally was a tall man only slightly stooped by his seventy-plus years. Thin white hair almost covered his freckled scalp. Given to wearing serviceable blue pants and sturdy work shirts, his jangling keys were his only fashion statement.

Wally made us feel welcome with a cup of coffee and a bit of chat as he swept the floors and began polishing toddler fingerprints off the heavy plateglass doors.

A few months later, we joined the church and, in the course of things, I started teaching Sunday school. Wally was the one I turned to when I needed an extension cord, a mop, or access to the locked supply closet.

As a teacher, I quickly learned that any lesson goes better if the art project has glitter. In the ten years I taught, my classes scattered the stuff like slug trails from the balcony to the base-ment. Wally never raised an eyebrow; he just went to work with his broom.

For Wally's seventy-fifth birthday, the church threw him a party. He was gracious, as always, but uncomfortable too. He wasn't used to being the center of attention. When it was over, he went home, changed clothes, and came back to fold up the tables and clean up the mess.

A few years later I took on the job of wedding coordinator. Through hundreds of weddings, Wally was on call. Whenever the coffeemaker wouldn't perk, candles couldn't be found, or toilets overflowed—Wally would save the day.

The rainy summer before the church was re-roofed, Wally and I spent a lot of Saturdays putting buckets beneath leaks and trying to make them look like part of the wedding decor. That was the year the ring bearer threw up in the first pew and the organist forgot the key to the organ. Wally was always there with his smile and his key ring.

Last year, Wally's health began to fail. It was time for his assistant John to take over.

Wally went from the hospital to a nursing home, and he came to church for services when he was well enough. But he was no longer there to unlock the doors first thing every morn-ing, and someone else closed up at night.

That summer there were weddings every weekend. Some time along the way, I lost my key. At the church office, John opened the key box. "I think this was Wally's," he said, as he handed me a replacement. My throat closed up and my eyes welled with tears.

A few months later, at the age of eighty-eight, Wally died. At the viewing, Wally's tool belt and overalls were displayed with his hammers and saws. They told the story of the quiet worker he was.

Wally has turned in his keys here, but I can just see him in heaven standing in the back, holding a broom. He won't be the center of attention. He'll be the one sweeping the floors and polishing the banisters. He'll see that the tables are set up for the banquets and that every light shines.

And down here, we will all remember him as Wally, the Earth Angel who opened doors for everyone.

"At Any Time . . ."

Chelene Reiley • *26* • *Store Manager*

I was a camp counselor for several years. I had gone to camp as a kid, and I remembered each of my counselors. I wanted the opportunity to help make camp memorable for the kids the way my counselors had for me.

One particularly challenging year, I had about a dozen kids in my group. One was an autistic boy named Justin, and I think he was eleven years old. I was looking forward to working with him, because I felt it would be a good learning experience for me.

Justin was a very anxious child. He was especially concerned about what might happen, as he put it, "at any time."

For example, we held a Circus Day with lots of decorations and balloons, and Justin seemed very nervous. I asked him what was wrong, and he said, "It's the balloons. At any time they could pop. I don't know when that might happen."

Over the summer I could see that his mind was going five hundred miles a minute, always worrying about what *might* happen:

"At any time, our bus could stop."

"At any time, you could stop paying attention to me."

"At any time . . ."

I spoke with Justin's counselor from home about his concerns. The counselor felt that Justin needed to feel some sense of control.

So I gave him a needle, and told him, "At any time, *you* could *make* the balloon pop."

I tried to look for situations where Justin could *make* something happen. I also began to tease him good-naturedly, in an effort to help him lighten up.

"At any time . . . ," I'd say to him, ". . . at any time, I could HUG you!"

I knew Justin hated to be hugged or touched in any way. "No!" he'd say. "No!" We joked like that for the rest of the summer.

I wasn't sure whether I had made any impression on Justin, until the last day of camp. We were riding home on the bus, and we came to his stop. He got up to leave, then he turned to me and said, "At any time . . ."

I smiled and said, "At any time . . ."

And he said, "At any time, I could HUG you!" Then he ran up to me and gave me a big hug. It was the only time he had ever hugged me.

Then he was off, up the hill toward his house. That was the last time I saw him.

My Earth Angel, Justin, made *me* believe what I had been trying to teach *him*. Though something bad could happen "at any time," something good could happen just as easily.

Chapter 2

Our Family,
Our Earth Angels

If you ever find happiness by hunting for it,
you will find it as the old woman did—
safe on her nose all the time.

—*Josh Billings*

One rainy day, we found a surprise in our mailbox. Among all the bills and junk mail was a personal-looking white envelope addressed to "Earth Angels." There was no return address.

As we walked back into the house, we tried to figure out who had sent it. After all, we had set up an Earth Angels post office box, so how did someone know our home address?

We sat on the couch with this mysterious envelope and began to open it. Much to our surprise, we found a submission from a member of our family! No wonder Mom had sent it to our home.

Most of us expect our family members to be our Earth Angels, so we sometimes take them for granted and assume that they already know how we feel.

While listening to these stories and reading this special one of our own, we were reminded of how important it is to let those who are closest to us know how we feel. After interviewing these people, many of them told us they had shared something that they had never before expressed, and we found ourselves encouraging them to share their story with family members.

We recently attended our grandfather's eighty-fifth birthday celebration. It was a wonderful opportunity for everyone to let him know how much he means to them, and what a significant and special role he has played in their lives.

On our drive home, we talked about how good it felt to express our emotions and how watching his reacton felt even better. But, we asked ourselves, why should it take a momentous occasion to tell him these things?

Every day is an opportunity to let our family members know

how much we appreciate them for being in our lives and to thank them for all that they do for us. Why not give someone a gift they can carry with them, rather than a eulogy they will never hear.

Don't be surprised if after reading the stories in this chapter, you find yourself picking up the phone, writing a letter, or walking into the other room to share a gift of your own with your loved ones.

I Have Three

Esther Biederman • 73 • Mother and Writer

You say you are lucky to have found someone who cares enough about you to be there for you? What if you had three!

I have three children who are far more than mere offspring. Several years ago their father died. And since that depressing and sad day, they have probably saved my life. Each day I get a phone call from one or more of them. They are here to take me out to dinner, a movie, shopping, or a visit to their home. There is always some special event they want me to attend with them. Never mind that they have families of their own who need their

attention, their love and devotion has never faltered. It's difficult—it's not enough—to just say thank you.

I know one thing for sure—they are my three angels here on
earth. How could anyone ask for more?

Grannie's Back Door

Melba Buxton Taylor • *78* • *Retired Teacher*

During the depression years of the twenties and thirties,
many hobos, adrift, penniless, and hungry, congregated
near the watering tanks on the Union Pacific Railroad in make-
shift shelters. Since my Grannie Burwell's house was the closest
in sight, they seemed to beat a path to her door to ask for a
handout. It was as if they all knew an Earth Angel lived there.

One day, as Grandpa sat down for lunch, a knock came at
the back door, and Grannie hurried to answer it.

"What can I do for you?"

"Well, ma'am, I'd be obliged if you'd let me cut some kin-
dling or do some other chores for a bite to eat. I sure am hungry."

"All right, you go to the pump there and wash up a bit, and
I'll fix you a plate of stew and some warm bread. Then we'll see
what I can find for you to do."

"Thanks, ma'am, sure be kind of you."

Grannie soon dished him up a big portion of food and carried it out to the porch. Grandpa watched patiently, as usual.

The next day, Grandpa sat down for lunch and, again, came a knock at the door. Grannie answered the door and was startled to see a young boy's face.

"Well, son, you look mighty tuckered and tattered, and skinny as a rail. What can I do for you?"

The lad dropped his eyes to his frayed shoes and stammered, "I . . . I . . . I need a drink of water."

"Gosh, it looks like you could do with more than water. How about some sandwiches and a glass of milk, and maybe a piece of pie if I can find some?"

He opened his mouth in disbelief. His eyes lit up with surprise as he swallowed and nodded, "Yes'm."

"Well, you sit there a minute and I'll get you some warm water and a towel so you can clean up a bit while I fix you a bite."

Soon she was back with a basin, soap, and towel, and a clean but slightly oversized shirt.

"Thanks. You didn't need to do all this," he choked out as she went back to fix him a plate.

She returned with the sandwiches and milk, which he tackled with gusto. Grannie sat down beside him and began her conversation.

"What's your name?"

"Jim."

"Jim? Where did you come from, Jim?"

"Akron, Ohio."

"All that way alone on the trains?"

He blinked and nodded, "Yes'm."

"Does your mama know you're here, Jim?" she asked softly.

Jim looked away and down at his shoes again. His mouth quivered as he said, "Yes, she knows."

"You sure? 'Cause if she doesn't, I bet she's worried sick about where you've gone to. How long have you been gone?"

"Eight days, I think." A tear slid out of his eye and he swiped his sleeve across his face.

"Well, I'm going to bring you some paper and a pencil out here after I get you some pie, so you can write her a note, and we'll mail it on for you."

"No. No. She ain't worrying."

"By now, I bet she is." Grannie rose and went inside. She walked to the wall phone and rang up the sheriff.

"Sheriff Ed? This is Emma Burwell and I've got a youngster here off the tracks. He can't be more than twelve or thirteen years old. Says he's from Akron, Ohio. I'm sure he's a runaway kid. Think you can come get him and we'll get a ticket back home for him?"

"Sure thing, Em. Hold him 'til I get there."

"Okay. I'll see about finding him some more clothes and try to get him to take a bath."

Grandpa asked, "What's going on? What's all that about?"

"Well, Harry, I know that kid's a runaway. Hasn't got any soles on his shoes and probably hasn't eaten a meal since he left Akron eight days ago. Why don't you fix your plate and eat, while I tend him?"

Grandpa shook his head and gathered up some lunch for himself.

Jim, with a full stomach and clean clothes, was soon admitting to Grannie that he was, in fact, a runaway and wanted to go back, but was too scared. Grannie assured him he'd be better off home and that things would work out for him. Sheriff Ed arrived and the three talked things over.

"Well, Jim, you're lucky you found this lady. Now I'll take you to the depot and buy you a ticket home. How's that?"

"Fine," his voice quavered. "I guess maybe they have been looking for me."

"All right, I'll call the sheriff in Akron. He can get in touch with your mom and meet your train and take you home. Now, let me see you smile."

"Okay," Jim grinned.

Grandma gave him a sack lunch and a big hug before they left for the depot.

The next day, lunchtime came and Grannie, again, answered the door at the knock.

There stood Grandpa.

"What are you doing standing there knocking?" she demanded.

"Well, I've discovered this is the surest, quickest way to get something to eat around here, Lady Bountiful," he laughed, as the screen door closed behind him and he made his way to the table.

Welcome Home Tiffany

Tiffany Suzanne Sanford · 21 · Student

I want to tell the world about my Earth Angel. He is one of the warmest, kindest, most intelligent, strong, creative, expressive, and enthusiastic people I have ever known. He has made an indelible impression on my life. In fact, without him, I would have no life. He is none other than my wonderful dad, Frank Sanford.

I guess there are lots of women out there who would say that their dad is the greatest, but mine is truly exceptional. He is a big, warm, protective man who works as an electrician. He took up this trade because he wanted a reliable source of income so he could provide for his family.

He is severely dyslexic, so reading and writing are difficult for him. When he was young, he was often told he was stupid; as a result, he was not encouraged in scholarly pursuits. I always thought he would have been a great lawyer or politician, since he's very eloquent.

One of my fondest childhood memories is of bath night and bedtime. My mom would give my sister and me a bath, and my dad would tap dance into the bathroom, singing a song he'd made up called "Shampoo Man." We would laugh and laugh as he washed our hair.

Then we'd get tucked into bed and our mom would read us a story. In lieu of reading, Dad would *tell* us a story. He made up a continuing saga which he called "Sean, The Wonder Dog, and Francine Tucker." This tale changed every night, and my sister and I always had a role to play in the action. The story went on for years!

My dad loves Christmastime. Every year my sister and I get a special gift just from him; one that he has picked out himself. Each Christmas morning we have to go through a ritual in which me, my mom, and my sister stand in the hallway while Dad gets the video camera ready. Then he videotapes us as we come running around the corner so that he can see the looks on our faces when we see our presents under the tree. (My sister and I are now nineteen and twenty-one, and we still do this!)

One Christmas Eve Dad sneaked out of the house before church. When he came back, he had beautiful corsages for us, his three girls! He has always made Christmas so memorable.

I lived through a very scary episode when I was a child. I was in the eighth grade and had to be admitted to the hospital because I had a mysterious stomach problem that prevented me from keeping down any food or water. They eventually determined that I needed an operation. By the time I went into surgery, I had lost twenty-five pounds. As I was wheeled into the operating room, I had a parent on each side saying, "I love you! I love you!"

When I regained consciousness, my mom was there, and I asked her what was wrong with me. She said, "You had a tumor, honey." I asked her if it was cancer, and she said "No." Relieved, I fell back to sleep. When I woke up again, my room was filled with flowers and balloons!

My parents took turns visiting with me in the hospital. One night my dad had an important talk with me. He told me that I had to get up and walk, that it would help me get better faster. So I dragged my skinny little body out of the bed, and, with my intravenous stand dragging behind, he helped me walk. He whispered, "I didn't know if I was ever going to see you walk again. I didn't know if I'd ever dance with you at your wedding. I don't know what I would have done if we'd lost you."

A few days later I was released from the hospital. On the way home I saw a giant banner hanging from a freeway overpass that read: "WELCOME HOME TIFFANY!" Once again my thoughtful dad had made an occasion special. He made me feel loved and important.

He has always made me believe that I am capable of doing anything. I've never said all this to my dad, and I'm not sure he even knows how much I notice everything he does and how much it matters to me. I want him to read this and know that he is my Earth Angel.

I wish everyone in the world could have one hour's worth of the love I've gotten from my dad.

Truest of the Blue

Michelle • *32* • *Systems Analyst*

Jeff and I have been friends since we were children. When I was eleven, our parents had an argument that ended their friendship for ten years. Jeff and I didn't see each other or talk during all that time.

When I was twenty-one and Jeff was twenty-three, his father died. My mother decided it was time to mend the differences; she wanted to be with her friend during this difficult time. I went to their house with my mom after the funeral. Our mothers hugged and cried.

When I saw Jeff, I noticed how grown up he was. I looked up at him and didn't know what to say. I just took his hand and he seemed to know how I felt. Jeff was much too young to lose his father.

We have remained good friends since then; Jeff is the older

brother I always wanted. I turn to him often for advice or just a hug.

Six years ago Jeff's mother found out that she had cancer. Jeff, his older brother, and his younger sister became much closer as they began to deal with this disease. Suddenly the tables were turned and they had to take care of their mother.

I have watched how they stay by her and care for her, especially Jeff. If she doesn't want to be alone, Jeff will sleep in the hospital room with her. He hardly leaves her side. He also sold his house and moved back in with her. He has been there every step of the way—driving her to chemotherapy, holding her hand, and making her laugh.

Recently Jeff's mom had to have two more surgeries at UCLA Medical Center. Each time the cancer returns, there is more fear. One important lesson the family has learned is to live for today.

Jeff heard that the Los Angeles Dodgers were having a "Truest of the Blue" contest. It's a contest where people write in explaining what makes them the best fan. The winners get a full Dodgers uniform and are invited to spend the day at the ballpark. Knowing how special this would be to his mom, since she was such a fan, Jeff wrote the following letter on her behalf:

To whom it may concern:

I am writing this letter on behalf of my mother, Hannah, the Truest of the Blue.

In 1990, my mom was diagnosed with ovarian cancer. This

particular disease is insidious and very difficult to cure. Since her first diagnosis, she has undergone six major surgeries and five chemotherapy treatments. This includes her latest bout, which she is fighting at this very moment.

I believe my mom's story makes her the Truest of the Blue, because her life and her fight mirror the values of the Los Angeles Dodgers and Major League Baseball.

When my mom first immigrated to this country in 1952 at the age of fourteen, she quickly realized that the best way to learn the American culture was to immerse herself in baseball. This, of course, endeared her to many teenage boys who seized the opportunity for a date and a baseball game in the same evening.

Once, years later, she even got kicked out of the stands for yelling at a Yankee pitcher—just weeks before giving birth to her first child.

She raised us kids (my older brother, me, and my younger sister) to bleed Dodger Blue. Many of our fondest childhood memories revolve around family outings at the ballpark. My mother made sure that baseball was a part of our lives.

One of the best therapies throughout her ordeal has been her beloved Dodgers. She watches games from her hospital bed, recuperates while listening to the radio, and always talks about getting better so she can once again go to the stadium and take in a game.

Her courage and strength continue to be a great source of inspiration to her family and friends. This is the greatest gift she can give us.

My mother has taught us about courage and loyalty, passion and sportsmanship. I believe my mom is the Truest of the Blue because she is a living example of the best of what the Dodgers are about.

—Jeff

Hannah *was* chosen as the Truest of the Blue—because of Jeff's letter. While she was recovering from another surgery, Jeff sat by her bed and quietly handed her the letter he had written. Hannah had tears in her eyes as she hugged and thanked her son for his thoughtful words. Then he read the letter he received that day from the Dodgers. She reached for him again and this time she hugged him with all of her strength.

It seemed Jeff had given her something wonderful to look forward to. I don't think he realized, at the time, that what he had done would help speed her recovery, but she was determined to be strong enough to walk, by herself, out onto the field to show her pride in a game that, to her, represented the spirit of America.

Jeff was worried that she wouldn't be strong enough to go, but the morning of the event, Hannah seemed to have more energy than she had had in a long time. This was the first time she had gotten out of the house in a couple of months, and they had a great time.

The Dodgers gave Hannah a "Dodger Blue" uniform, which she wore that evening as she stood on the field in front of a stadium full of people. She was able to talk to, and take pictures with, the coach and team members. It was a wonderful memory the whole family will always keep in their hearts.

I feel that Jeff is an Earth Angel, not because he is a son who takes care of his mother, but because his unselfish devotion goes beyond a son's duties. It seems that sometimes we are tested in life, and our endurance is pushed to such a limit that, if we prevail, we emerge with wings.

Quinceñera—*A Passage to Womanhood*

Carol Martinez • 16 • Goal: Parole Officer

M y dad would always hug me when he saw me crying. He would come home from work, kiss us on our foreheads, and ask if we were hungry. Every night he would come into our room and tuck in me and my sister.

It was very important to him that we go to school. He would often tell us his story about coming to America for work and how hard it was for him to cross the border. He didn't want us to end up in the fields picking strawberries or celery.

Soon I was going to graduate from junior high. It would be a very special day. My dad would tell me that he was proud of me for staying in school so that I could grow up and be somebody. I knew that on my graduation day I would be really happy, because I would make him proud.

To add to my happiness, my dad told me that he was going to make me a *quinceñera* in two months. A *quinceñera* is a big party given for a girl when she turns fifteen. It's an important day when she is presented to the community as an adult. It's kind of like a sweet sixteen. What would make it even more special was that my dad said he would give a speech in front of my friends and relatives saying how proud he was to present me as a young woman. He would also dance a waltz with me and give me my last doll before I reached womanhood.

All was well until one night, just before my *quinceñera*, when my dad crashed his car into a telephone pole and died instantly. I think you can imagine how my family and I felt. I just wanted him back.

Now, one year later, I consider my dad, Alfonso V. Martinez, my Earth Angel. He was a great man, and before he died, he had typed and left a letter in our computer. It was the speech that he was going to say to me the day of my *quinceñera*. Nobody knew he had typed it until I found it. Through that letter he came back to me. It read, "I'm so proud of Carol and I thank God for letting us share this special day together." Even though I couldn't hear his voice, I could read about how proud he was of me and, most of all, I could feel his love.

I will treasure that letter and the memories of my father forever. (May my father rest in peace.)

Growing Up with Mrs. Claus

E. M. O'Donnell • *33* • *Environmental Publications Consultant*

I can't think of any real-life person who comes closer to the spirit of giving embodied in Mrs. Claus than my mother. Ever since I can remember, she was always giving things away. I'm sure all of my siblings recall conversations that went something like this: "Hey Mom, have you seen my _____ ?'' (Fill in the blank with: shirt, sweater, bat, jacket, or any other object that would fit in a box.)

A momentary silence before the reply would indicate that it wasn't simply our own carelessness at fault this particular time. The dreaded answer would then inevitably come: "Oh! That old thing? You never used it anyway, so I sent it to _____ .'' (Fill in the blank with: the Salvation Army, the Purple Heart, Goodwill, etc.)

Pleas like, "But Mom! I only wore those boots three times!'' never seemed to stem the outward flow of you-name-it from our household.

While we were growing up, the first Saturday of every month meant newspaper drives. My father was behind the wheel, and my brothers and I would scamper in and out, tossing the bundles into the back of our aging Chevy wagon.

My mother's pattern of community concern continued well into my college days. But by then, because we kids were out of the house, she focused her efforts on two other areas: dogs and junk. As children, we always had pets around. There were usually several resident dogs and fish, and at times even a few turtles and ducks. However, it seemed that once the word got out in canine circles that my mother was taking in strays, a new four-footed friend would appear at my parents' door each week.

Of course, my mother wouldn't hear of her friends and relatives leaving their dogs at kennels while they went on vacation, so at times, when I was home for a visit, there would be as many as ten dogs there, and I would have to elbow my way in for a spot by the fire.

In time, my mother increased her collecting and redistributing efforts. Huge quantities of used clothing and household goods began filling the empty spaces of my parents' modest suburban home. Before passing things on, she would mend tears, scrub stains, wash, iron, sort, label, and pack it all off to those in need.

Over the years, my folks also sent many packages overseas—clothes, books, toys, tools, and towels—to places I had never even heard of.

Perhaps because of the many tales I was told of kids starving in Africa, I joined the Peace Corps after college and spent two years in West Africa.

My mother looked on this as a newfound opportunity to send even more things overseas, and she expanded her operations accordingly. My mother was becoming an Earth Angel to thousands of people whom she would never meet.

When my brother and uncle visited me at my rural post, they brought a very large sack of stuff from home for the people in my village. As I began handing things out to different villagers, my brother exclaimed, "Hey, that's my T-shirt!" A moment later he added, "And that's my hat!" and so on until all had been given out. As we watched the once-familiar items go off with their new owners, my brother and I smiled at each other knowingly. Evie had struck again!

After my father retired, my parents' volunteer efforts took on a life of their own. Now, in addition to a constant stream of dogs, clothes, and broken items, they "do" food. That is, each weekend my father drives his station wagon (which now has over two hundred thousand miles on it) around to local businesses and grocery stores and collects leftover food items that would otherwise be thrown out. Together, he and my mother sort, pack, and label the food, which he then takes to the soup kitchen in the city, where he volunteers each Sunday.

One Sunday, when I accompanied my father to the soup kitchen, I overheard one of the new volunteers tell him, "No sir, you have to sit in the dining room with the other guests." I looked up at him consolingly. Perhaps if Mom hadn't given away his new sweater, I thought, he wouldn't look like a street person.

I was returning, during the holidays, from another trip to East Africa, where I had gone to join a Habitat for Humanity building project. I had left some gear and my dog (one more barely makes a difference) at my folks' place. When I walked in the door to their house, I remarked, "It looks like a permanent garage sale in here." I proceeded to make my way through the boxes and excess furniture. My dog, who came bounding through the debris to greet me, looked suspiciously heavier.

The next morning, before I left, I gathered my things together and packed my car. "Hey Mom," I said, hesitantly, "I can't find my new blue hiking boots. I thought I left them in the closet. Have you seen them?"

I knew from her silent reply that they were gone, destined for some other size 8½ feet, perhaps in Appalachia. So I gave her a kiss on the cheek and said, "I know if I were in my shoes right now, I would be grateful the world has a Mrs. Claus. And I'm glad she's my mother." Then she gave away something she would always have in abundance—a big hug packaged especially for me.

On my drive home, I looked over at my contented, well-fed pooch, and thought to myself, *Good thing Mom doesn't give away dogs . . .*

She's the One

Steven Daniels • 14 • Goal: Sports Doctor or Attorney

She's the one who is always there for me even when not
asked.
She's the one who encourages me to do better.
She's the one who tells me to practice when I get cut from
the baseball team.
She's the one who helps me with algebra homework, even
when she is exhausted from a long day at work.
She's the one who lets me know when I am acting like a jerk.
She's the one who tells me to ignore people who give me a
hard time for getting better grades than they do.
She's the one who puts up with my behavior.
She's the one who takes me to the doctor when I'm ill.
She's the one who will do anything for my good fortune.
She's the one who gives up her leisure time to take me to
soccer practice.
She's the one who has a shoulder I can cry on.
She's the one who understands me and my fears.
She's the one who gets the cheap shoes so I can have the best
shoes.
She's the one who told me what drugs can do to you.
She's the one who encourages me not to be afraid of some-
one bigger.

She's the one who bought the pen for me to write this poem.
She's the one who does everything for me.
She is the mom you see on TV and wish she was your mom.
She is the one I am thankful for every day.
She is the one I call my Earth Angel.
She is my mom.

Boubameisas

Stacy Savran Penzer • 25 • Children's Book Editor

"I know a story about three little boys," my grandmother used to say. I'll always remember the first time I heard it . . .

"One was so handsome and smart all the girls in school loved him." (That was our father, Billy.) "One was tall and sweet, and never put up a fuss." (That was Uncle Jeffrey.) "And one got all the attention by banging on his drums and getting into mischief." (That was Uncle Stevie.)

"These three boys," she continued, "loved their mother so much that they decided to do something very special for her one day. So you know what they did? Well, one afternoon when they came home from school, she was fast asleep and snoring soundly. Tiptoeing around the house, they snuck into her bedroom and took two tubes of lipstick and a stick of pink rouge from her dresser. Then, the mischievous one began giggling and they raced out of the room.

"When their mother woke from her nap, she could hear her sons whispering in the next room, their feet shuffling on the carpet. 'Boys! I'm up!' she shouted, and suddenly there was silence.

"Getting a funny feeling, she got up to see what was going on. At first all she saw were the sheepish grins on the three faces that matched the color of the red carpet. Then she noticed the walls.

"Can you guess what covered the walls?" Grandmother asked.

"Lipstick!" I guessed, horrified yet thrilled.

"And rouge!" called out my sister, Jennifer.

"Yessiree!" said Nana. "You see these wooden panels covering the walls? If we took them down you would see that it still says WE LOVE YOU MOM in red lipstick and pink rouge."

"Wow! Your sons must really love you," Jennifer said.

"Absolutely," said Nana. "That's why I never washed the walls and instead put up the wooden panels—to preserve it forever."

"Is that a true story, Nana?" I asked.

"No, Stace-ele. It's only a *boubameisa*. Now, let me tuck you in."

"What's a *boubameisa*?"

"A fib, something made up, pretend. Now goodnight, sleep tight!"

Usually, after Nana's stories, I was able to go right to sleep. But not that time. I was up all night wishing I could rip the panels off the walls.

As a grandmother, Vivian (aka Nana) took her job very seriously. After raising three sons, she was delighted to have granddaughters. Luckily, I came along first. She frequently sang "Thank Heaven for Little Girls" to me. I was special to her, and she made sure I knew it.

For two blissful years I had Nana all to myself. Then Jennifer was born, but it became clear that Nana cherished both of us equally and uniquely.

As we grew, Jennifer and I needed what most grandchildren need—songs, junk food, games, and the outdoors—all of which were endlessly supplied. For Jennifer, the budding actress, Nana dressed up in fancy clothes (like her bathrobe), letting us paint (smear) her face and curl (yank) her hair. For me, the budding amateur chef, Nana spent endless hours sifting flour, braiding challah dough, and frying potato pancakes.

Inevitably, the first stop at Nana's was the candy drawer. Mysteriously, only peanuts could be found in the boxes of Cracker Jacks, and more than one Mallomar always seemed to be missing its Mallo. We'd sit at the kitchen table chomping on chocolate-covered cherries, and we'd play "Go Fish" or "Steal the Old Man's Bundle." At those times, more than any other, life was sweet.

But life wasn't always a bowl of chocolate-covered cherries

for Vivian, and maybe that's why she appreciated those sweet little things so much. Vivian Schweid was raised by Russian immigrants, and she held on dearly to old-world values.

Of all the rooms in her house, the kitchen was her sanctuary. Everyone within smelling distance was put in a trance and lured there, especially on Sunday morning. Those who were fortunate enough to sleep over would wake to the most comforting, intoxicating aroma. Nana called it her "Sunday Spread."

I have made a vow to continue her Sunday tradition (once I have an apartment big enough to have more than one guest).

I loved her cooking but, even more, I loved hearing her stories.

When I was fifteen, Nana died. I never got the chance to say good-bye, and at that time, I couldn't have expressed what she meant to me. Only in retrospect have I truly begun to appreciate and understand how deeply Vivian affected my life.

At my wedding last year, I felt an overwhelming absence. My paternal grandparents had never gotten the chance to meet Eric, whom they would have loved as I do, and who embodies every value they held dear. But I now realize that Nana and Grandpa *were* there—in the kiddush cup, under the *chupah*, on top of the cake, in their three sons, in the flower girl (my cousin Valerie, Vivian's namesake), and in my new husband's eyes.

There are many things that can be said about Nana. She was old-fashioned. She liked the Rockettes, jumping over waves in the ocean, walking the boardwalk on Coney Island, taking the train, eating Cracker Jacks, singing songs, kneading dough, and being with her family.

To say I would have grown up just the same without her—well, that would be the biggest *boubameisa* of them all.

A Space of My Own

Donna McGuire Tanner • *49* • *Freelance Writer*

My Granddad McGuire was much like any other grandparent. Being a hard-working father of seven, he had to be somewhat skilled at everything from carpentry to farming. In a time when living off the land and life without modern conveniences was the norm, one thing set my grandfather apart from others. He was what most people would have called "handicapped." But he did not allow himself to be labeled as such.

It's strange, but until I was about eight years old, I was oblivious to his condition. I suppose it's because, to me, that was the way he always was. When he was four years old he fell, hands first, into a fireplace. His right hand was to remain, forever, in an almost permanent clutch. On his left hand, he had a thumb and a stiff index finger; the rest of the fingers were set in an immovable downward position. Most people recoiled when they looked at these hands.

For a few days, after I realized that Granddad's hands were not normal, I positioned my hands like his, and I tried to pick things up or just hold something. I found that even simple chores were impossible, yet he had always made using his hands look so easy and natural.

Granddad was a religious man, and he did not focus on the negative side of his accident. Instead he felt grateful that God had pulled him from certain death. My most vivid memory is of him at the dinner table with his hands together as he said "Grace."

I remember watching him at work on the farm. He could plant seeds, hoe, and harvest crops. After he cut the hay, I helped him stack it. With a horse and sleigh, he went into the woods to gather firewood, sometimes letting me go with him. After loading the sleigh, he would lift me onto the horse or leave space on the sleigh for me to ride home.

Grandma made sure that he didn't get out of pitching in with household chores. He helped her with the cooking and canning, and after Sunday supper, he always drafted me to help him do the stacks of dirty dishes. First we carried in water from a well, then we heated it on a woodstove in the kitchen. I always suspected that he picked me to help because I washed while he dried; he hated washing the buttermilk glasses.

Granddad was a soft-spoken man. He had many grandchildren but tried not to show favoritism as he didn't want to spark rivalry among us. I knew he was wise, and I felt he understood me better than anyone else did. There were seven children in my family and my own special identity was often suffocated.

Space was a rare commodity. Every Sunday, in an over-crowded car, we would make our thirty-mile trip to my grand-parents' farm near Ansted, West Virginia. One day, as we arrived at their home, I was in the middle of a confrontation with my younger brothers. They had again found my diary and read it! It didn't hold many secrets, but it was personal and the only space I had.

Grandma and Granddad were used to family disputes. They were as sure it would pass as I was that it wouldn't. The next Sunday was supposed to be the same as any other, but it was destined to touch my life forever. When I walked into my grandparents' house, they were both grinning at me. Granddad went onto the back porch and, when he returned, in his crip-pled hands was a box. He had made it out of pieces of scrap wood; it was painted gold and had a green lid. Using old copper tubing, he had fashioned handles for the sides. On the front was a padlock. The box was just the right size for my treasures. Granddad held it down so I could see the top: in big bold letters he had written my name.

I now had a space of my own.

Today the box remains my most prized possession. When-ever I feel despair, all I have to do is look at it. My Earth Angel will always have his very own space in my heart.

Maby Baby

Stacee King • *28* • *Freelance Script Reader for Movie Studios*

There was never a first time I met Mabel. She had always just been there. She would engulf me in her huge bosom and the starch of her uniform would scratch my cheek.

She ironed in the laundry room off the kitchen where the warm smell of freshly pressed clothes seeped out. I was a little princess in frilly dresses who could never resist the sloppy puddle of mud in the garden. She would tell me not to get dirty, but I ignored her pleas, so she was always bathing, braiding, powdering, and dressing me. We played while the clothes dried. Prideful, she would present me clean to my grandfather, knowing full well that I couldn't wait to muddy myself again.

She smiled when I talked of school. She frowned when I described my loneliness. She understood.

Driving to or from the park, my brother and I would laugh in the back seat of her car and yell, "Maby Baby!" She would try not to laugh. Her mouth pursed, her forehead creased, she would say, "You kids have to calm down." One time we threw soda cans out the window and she got mad; it lasted for about three minutes. It was the only time I remember her getting mad. She still laughed. She understood kids.

One day my grandparents had a party. I smiled, charmed, and pleased like a good little girl but I couldn't wait to get back to Mabel. I snuck back to the laundry room where she was with the other servants. I had them all laughing. She proudly looked on. She held me with her eyes, and my heart felt safe.

When it was time for bed, I said my good-nights and kissed everyone. She took me to my room, and, standing in the doorway after turning off the lights, said, "I love you."

Years passed and I started to date. Mabel was the one who told me I was special and shouldn't settle for what's-his-name.

Mabel died when I was twenty-six. For twenty-two years my Earth Angel had been hidden in the laundry room.

At her funeral, I stood tall and spoke to a church filled with her family and friends. After a powerful statement, they rejoined with, "Yes! Oh yes!" Their eyes shined brightly as I spoke of her great heart. Her enormous body was a house for pure and honest love; a love that knew no racial boundaries; a love that transcended social positions; a love that taught, understood, cherished, and kept safe a little girl who was sometimes scared and alone. Yes! A love so great it was otherworldly.

As I described the woman who had helped form my heart and spirit, I looked out at her family—a group of strangers, and yet they were people with whom I shared a common love. I recognized in them Mabel's great capacity for laughter, joy, and love.

On the Street Where He Lives

Melvin • 14 • Goal: Architect

My Earth Angel is a nice person. He has an old face, but a young personality. We don't live together, but he sees me every day when I walk down Saviers Road.

He is my dad.

When my mom passed away I was only ten. My dad didn't take it very well and that's when his problems started. He began to drink a lot and couldn't support us anymore, but he made sure I was okay by taking me to live with my grandparents. I guess he couldn't handle living without my mother.

Even though we don't live with each other, he has still helped me a lot through life. We are just like friends, and inside we know we really love each other. He likes me for me and I like him for him.

My dad lives in a little shack and doesn't have a good job. He does different small jobs like painting houses and doing plumbing, but they don't pay enough for a real home.

Although he is poor, I let people know he is my father. He doesn't hurt me and he listens to my problems. My dad helps me with my homework. He's always asking, "How are you doing in school?" "Are you getting good grades?" "Do you need help with math or English?" "How are things at home?" Whenever I do need help, I go to him. He understands me and has a good ear. He always calls me his "buddy." If I have problems at home, he tells me to be kind to my grandma.

Even though he's on the street, I know where to find him. My dad is a nice guy and lives like a poor one. Like they say, the outside doesn't count—it is all about the inside. He struggles, but he never gives up. Because we don't live together, he has to work harder than other dads to be a good father to me.

That's why I'm so proud of him, and that's why my dad is my Earth Angel.

Don't You Forget It

Anna Christie • *44* • *Computer Analyst*

"Don't you forget it," he always said when I said, "I love you." What's the big deal? Why couldn't he just say he loved me too? Spry and cocky, even at eighty-one, my uncle was stubborn and sarcastic and harder than ever to get close to.

When we used to visit him summers or at Christmas, he'd be in his blue khakis and oily hat, spitting tobacco. He was the one who let his tomboy niece ride on the back of the truck pitching hay to the longhorns. He taught me how to shoot a BB gun, thin out the pollywogs in the pond, scare possum out of the feeders, and breed and doctor cattle.

We listened intently every Sunday during my visits, while my aunt played the church piano. He prayed then and before every meal. The words were so low and mumbled I couldn't understand them, but I think God got the message. At night he played a squealing fiddle in tune with my aunt's piano.

A ranch can be a cruel place for animals, but Uncle Burn showed me the beauty of the deer, he let me help birth a calf, nurse a sick duck, and discover the wonder of God's creations.

Uncle Burn was the only man I had ever been close to as a child. He was the father I dreamed of. He was forty-two when I was born. Envious of my friends who had dads, I always wanted to be a "daddy's girl." I settled happily for being an "uncle's girl."

He and my aunt had desperately wanted children, but fate had other plans. He was a man without a child; I was a girl without a father. Even though we were separated by half the state of Texas, I thought of him on every holiday, on his birthday, and especially on Father's Day. Always I would sign his cards, "I Love You," and each time, he would call and say, "Don't you forget it."

I learned early in life to put away grudges. After losing my father and four grandparents to overnight deaths, I knew life made no promises. You can never know when the last words will be. If my uncle was sick, I didn't want to take the chance that he would leave this world without talking with me. Regardless of my personal feelings, regardless of how much I needed him, he needed me more.

Once a strong, independent man, at eighty-one, Uncle Burn was now alone. He couldn't turn on the dishwasher, time the microwave, or start the washer for clean clothes. My aunt had done these things before she died two years ago; now he was lost in their old house and seldom ate meals at home. Fortunately there were plenty of widows who wanted to cook for my fiesty uncle. They had other things in mind, but I knew Uncle Burn would never marry again. He was devoted to Aunt Suz even after her death.

When he went into the hospital Mother said he needed our support, even though he was some six hundred miles away. I gave him a call.

"Uncle Burn, how are you feeling?"

"Fine. I'm going home today. False alarm. You can't have my money yet."

"Very funny. You're leaving the hospital today?"

"My blood pressure was acting up. They say I'm fine. I'll be down at the senior citizens' hall by supper. Those 'widders' can't live without me."

Through the telephone I could hear him spit, and it made me smile. I wondered how many spit cans the nurses had accidentally kicked over, just as I used to do.

"You might give the widows a break. I'm glad you're okay. I just wanted to check in with you. Enjoy your dinner. I love you."

"I love you too." Click. He was gone.

I stared at the phone in disbelief. He had said it. He had

actually said "I love you" to me, not his traditional—"Don't you forget it." I started to call back. No, I wouldn't make a big deal out of it.

It was later that evening that my mother called to say he had died.

"But he was going home today. What happened?"

"They say he had a blood clot. The funeral is the day after tomorrow. The drive is so far, you don't have to go. Nobody will say anything if you don't show."

It didn't matter if anyone else said anything. I know what my Earth Angel would have said . . .

"Don't you forget it."

Chapter 3

Earth Angels from
Out of the Blue

Happiness sneaks in through a door
you didn't know you left open.
                              —*John Barrymore*

As our search continued, the stories began coming to us, often without our having to ask. Strangers became eager to contribute, and their stories were like precious gifts falling into our laps.

One afternoon we were sitting in the waiting area at the pharmacy—along with what seemed like every other sick person in the San Fernando Valley—waiting to pick up a prescription. It was flu season and there was not enough help behind the counter. We figured we'd sit down and get a little book work done.

A man with a cute little girl in his arms came over and sat down next to us. When the little girl saw us, she smiled and shyly put her head on her father's shoulder. We began playing peek-a-boo and when her father realized his daughter was moving back and forth and giggling, he turned around.

We told him we were playing and that his daughter was adorable.

He smiled. "She's usually a little shy. Do you have any kids?"

"Not yet," we said simultaneously.

"I have a son who is eight, and this is Carmen. Tell them how old you are." She hid behind her father and giggled. "She's four," he said.

Then, looking down at our notebook, he asked, "What's Earth Angels?"

We told him a little about the book.

"I have a great story for you," he said with wide eyes.

Enrique's story and the other stories in this chapter illustrate how a stranger can instantly become a positive and important part of your life. As children, we are taught not to talk to strangers. When we become adults, we continue to avoid strangers—to avoid eye contact or conversation. We've all become too afraid. But just *because you don't know someone doesn't mean they have bad intentions. You never know when someone you don't know may lend you a helping hand or may need a hand from you. After all, you're a stranger too.*

When you see strangers in this new light, the world becomes much brighter. So the next time you see someone you don't know in line at the market, or in a crowded elevator, or on the bus, remember that they may become your Earth Angel or you may become theirs.

Ain't This the Life?

Enrique Vasquez • 27 • C.P.A.

When I was fifteen an amazing thing happened to me. My family had immigrated from Mexico a few years earlier and, besides going to school, I had to work to help support my brothers and sisters; I am the oldest of eight kids. My parents are very proud people and believe that hard work makes a person strong.

Every day, during the summer, I stood on the corner about a block from our apartment with a group of other men, young and old. We waited for someone to pass by looking for workers. I did everything from construction to garbage collecting to gardening.

My father had had a heart attack the year before and could not do physical labor. Instead, he worked as a cashier in the neighborhood market. Every evening, I would come home and my parents would thank me and tell my brothers and sisters how hard I had worked. Even if I came home without getting work, my parents told me they appreciated me for trying. They all treated me with so much respect it was difficult to complain. I was always fighting within myself because, I guess, I was a typical teenager. I wanted to be hanging out with my friends at the mall instead of working all the time.

One day I was standing on the corner waiting for work, when a white truck drove up and stopped in front of us. A tall guy with blond hair and tanned skin rolled down his window. He looked carefully at the group of men, as though he was looking for someone in particular. His eyes passed me and then returned.

"Hi, do you speak English?" His voice was very deep.

I nodded.

He smiled. "Are you sure?"

"Yes," I replied nervously. "My name is Enrique and I speak English."

"Great," he said. "Can you come with me until about seven o'clock tonight?"

"Yes, I can. I just have to let my parents know I will be late. Can I call them really fast from this phone booth?"

"Sure," he said. "Hurry, though, we have people waiting."

I called my parents, and then climbed into the back of the truck. The man jumped out of the car and stopped me. He extended his hand and said, "Enrique, my name is Dan. Why don't you sit in the front of the truck. It's way too hot back there and the truck has air-conditioning."

I climbed back down, shook his hand, and thanked him.

I remember the ride very well. Dan asked me all sorts of questions. A lot of them were about what I wanted to do with my life when I graduated from high school. I told him I had not really thought about it. I explained that it was hard enough— with seven brothers and sisters—just going to school and working.

It was a pretty long drive, and we finally stopped at a marina. It was a beautiful day, and there were many boats sailing on the water. The ocean was sparkling, and I couldn't take my eyes off the water. I don't think I had ever seen anything so beautiful.

Dan opened the door for me and I felt foolish. I didn't realize how mesmerized I had been by what I was seeing. We walked along a deck with boats docked on both sides, and I noticed that they all had names. We stopped at one and Dan said, "Here she is." I looked at the name on the back. It said, "Ain't This the Life?"

Dan called out, "Hey, where is everyone? You both still sleeping?"

A tall man who looked like Dan came out from below, and a woman with long brown hair followed. Dan introduced me to his brother—I can't remember his name—and his brother's wife. Dan told them I was a friend of his and that he had invited me to spend the day with them.

They shook my hand, and I gave Dan a confused look. I quietly asked if I could talk to him in private. "Sure," he said. Then he looked at his brother. "We're just gonna get some coffee to take along. Don't leave without us."

We started walking to a coffee shop on the dock. I really didn't know what to say; I tried to be casual. "So, uh," I muttered, "what kind of work did you want me to do today?"

Dan looked down at me and gave me a smile I will always remember. "Today is a special day," he said. "It is a day for you to enjoy yourself. When I was about your age, Enrique, my uncle took me out for the day. He told my mother he was taking me to school and we ended up spending the whole day fishing. He taught me that life should be fun—full of adventure and surprises. My uncle told me to enjoy life. And, because of him, I have."

Then he stopped and looked at me seriously. "Enrique, my uncle died last week." His eyes started to fill with tears.

I didn't know what to do so I just stood there listening.

"Yesterday morning I saw you waiting for work. I guess I'm being ridiculous, but I remembered what my uncle had done for me and I wanted to give that back to someone. I know this all sounds strange, and I hope it's okay with you. You just looked so serious, and I thought it might be fun for you to spend the day out on the ocean. Have you ever fished before?"

"No," I replied. I couldn't believe what was happening.

"Well, we're gonna fish today! Maybe you can catch enough to bring back to that big family of yours." He smiled again, brushed the hair away from his eyes, and patted my shoulder.

We spent the whole day out on the boat. He and his brother teased each other a lot, and at one point I remember laughing so hard my stomach hurt. I learned how to bait a hook and reel in a fish. We saw dolphins jumping out of the water, and Dan's sister-in-law made great tuna sandwiches for lunch. I told them that I would love to have a boat like this someday.

Dan said, "I'm sure you will. Just don't work so hard that you don't have time for fun."

I fell asleep in the car on the way home, and Dan nudged me. "Hey, guy, you're back."

I looked at him and rubbed my eyes. "Thank you," I said. "I had a great day."

"You just take care of yourself, hear?" he said, as he handed me a hundred-dollar bill. "For all your hard work today," he chuckled.

He must have noticed my expression, so he continued, "I wouldn't have caught that last fish without you."

"I can't accept this," I said. I tried to argue and give the money back, but he insisted.

"I know you're going to have your own boat someday. Maybe you could take *me* fishing." He extended his hand and I shook it hard.

"Thank you," I said, "I'll never forget you."

This was about twelve years ago. Since then, my parents were able to send me to college and I am now a C.P.A. I am married and have two children.

Every other Sunday I take my father and my eight-year-old son fishing on our little boat. Painted on the back are the words, "Aint This the Life II?" I guess you could say it's a tribute to my Earth Angel, Dan.

"God Bless"

Beth Engel • 15 • Goal: Architect

Standing outside Duke's (a hamburger joint), I had to make an urgent phone call home. The problem was, I had no money. I asked a few nicely dressed couples for some change, and they looked at me as if I were speaking a different language.

Sitting there for five minutes, I had time to think about life and about how selfish and self-centered people are. Just as I was about to lose all hope for mankind, a homeless lady walked up to me and handed me twenty cents.

She smelled of stale cigarette smoke and moldy socks. Her sweatshirt was pink; it had probably belonged to someone who had buried it at the bottom of their drawer; but, to her, it was a treasure.

When she first walked over, I thought she was going to ask me for money. But I guess she had seen my unsuccessful attempts, so she gave me hers.

Then, just as calmly as she had come, she left, not asking for a thank you or a favor in return.

I saw her a month later and gave her all the coins in my pocket. She accepted, with a half-toothless smile. I told her of the favor she had done for me a month earlier. I guess she heard me, though there was no reply except, "God Bless."

Good Luck Come In

Mary Greene • 13 • Student, American School in London

When I was little, I moved from Washington, D.C. to Japan, where it was very different and I felt like I didn't fit in. But there was one person who made me feel at home, though I only saw her once.

One day my whole family went to Setsubun, a bean-throwing festival at a Shinto shrine. Above us was a long platform decorated with red and white ribbon. Two men came onto the platform dressed as red and green ogres. Everybody began chanting, *fuku-wa uchi oni-wa soto*, which means "good luck come in, bad luck go out."

Then, men dressed in blue kimonos came out and started throwing bags of chips to the crowd. Everybody was jumping up to grab them. I also jumped, but I was too small, and, no matter how hard I tried, I couldn't get one. This disappointed me; everyone had a bag but me.

I walked around, pushing through the crowds, to see if a bag had dropped on the ground. It was then that my Earth Angel, an old Japanese lady wearing a colorful kimono, walked over to me and handed me her bag of chips. I believed she had given me luck.

What she did was not amazing, but to me, it was very special, because after that day, other good things began to come to me and I finally felt like I belonged.

Worth the Wait

Carole Lee Atkinson • *55* • *Computer Software Instructor*

It was an unusually hot day in January, so I decided to take my three-year-old to Orange Julius. We'd been running around and needed something cool to drink. It seemed that the rest of the city had the same idea. The line was long, but an Orange Julius was worth the wait.

So, there I was, standing in line, feeling hot and lightheaded, when all of a sudden everything went black.

I came to, hearing my own voice calling out for my daughter.

"I'm here, Mommy," she said softly.

"Your daughter's just fine," said a kind and calming voice.

I looked up to see the gentle face of a man in his late sixties.

"Are you feeling better?" he continued. "I'm glad I was able to catch you before you hit the ground."

I told him I was okay and thanked him. Then I sat up and put my daughter on my lap.

The gentleman handed me a cup of cold water and said, "You're pregnant, aren't you?"

"I don't think so," I said, somewhat taken aback.

"I have six children and I can tell when a woman is pregnant." He smiled a big, knowing smile that I will always remember.

He helped me to my feet and said, "Everything is going to be just fine."

As he walked away, I yelled, "Thank you."

I was hoping to have another child, but had been having trouble getting pregnant. For a number of reasons, I was sure he couldn't be right and that I might be coming down with the flu, or perhaps it was the heat and the long wait.

One week later, I learned that I *was* pregnant. This stranger had known even before I did.

In my third month, I began to have serious complications. I was terribly afraid, but then the man's voice came back to me: "Everything is going to be just fine."

Six months later, I had a healthy baby girl. We named her Lorin Michelle.

It's been over thirty years and I have never forgotten the comforting sound of that gentleman's voice. He was there at the right time to catch me and give me a special message as my Earth Angel.

A Stranger's Smile

Janeth Hernandez • 17 • Goal: Professional Photographer

My mother and I had been arguing the whole day without stopping. In the afternoon, she said we would be going to my grandma's house. Finally, after another argument, I got in the car.

During the fifteen-minute drive, all my mother did was yell at me. I kept quiet or tried to say something in my favor, but things seemed to get worse.

It seemed as if my life was falling apart. My self-esteem was really low and I thought that the best thing for everyone would be if I just left this world forever. I wanted to run away or kill myself.

As we were in the car, I was feeling worse than before. I couldn't hold it in any longer. I looked out the window, and I began to cry.

Through my tears, I saw a man sitting on a curb, but I didn't really pay any attention at first. Then, as we got closer to him, he smiled at me and, even though it was for a brief moment, I could see in his eyes a thing that seemed to say, "It's okay. I understand. Things will get better."

To me, his smile, and the look in his eyes, made me stronger and able to take anything. I had never seen that man before, but it seems as if he knew me and what I was going through.

Now, every time I feel bad, I remember my Earth Angel and his warm smile. Since I don't know him, the only way I can thank him is by sharing *my* smile.

Yellow Carnation

Jenny • 30 • Administrative Director

When I was a sophomore in college, I had a roommate who was gorgeous. She looked like Michelle Pfeiffer, only prettier. Heads turned when she walked down the street, and everyone treated her like gold.

I, a mere mortal woman, was fairly invisible around her.

We were walking to the campus one cold Boston afternoon, and as we approached the Student Union, a flower cart vendor reached out with a yellow carnation in his hand. I moved away, thinking it was meant for my friend. Without a word, he put the pretty flower in *my* hand. I smiled at him and looked down at my surprise gift. It was as if he was telling me that I, like the flower, was pretty—even though I was standing next to my beautiful roommate.

I think I was the only person on the street whom he'd given a flower to!

I still have the carnation, pressed into one of my photo albums, as a reminder of the kind Earth Angel who showed me that I wasn't invisible.

Who Will Buy?

Cesar • 17 • Flower Salesman

I've been blessed with a lot of Earth Angels in my life. I could tell you about the man on our block who buys Halloween costumes for kids who can't afford them. Or my best friend, Ricky, who's always there for me in hard times. I love my mom, and my baby sister is real special to me. She was a gift from God for me and Mom. I know it.

But there's someone special I want to tell you about. He's special because I don't know his name and I still can't figure out why he did what he did.

Have you ever seen those kids who stand out on the street corner selling flowers? Well, that's me. A purple van filled with buckets of flowers picks me up near my apartment, then picks up a bunch of other kids, and drops us off at different street corners that are busy with traffic or near office buildings.

The man driving the van is our regional supervisor and he's pretty tough. He has a system for counting money and the daily inventory of flowers. I guess because he's working with kids and has had some bad experiences, he has to watch us, so he doesn't get scammed. I don't take it personally when he asks me questions, but some of the kids don't like it much.

It's not as easy as you think to sell flowers. Our prices are good, better than at a flower store, but people are in a hurry and hardly see you standing there. A good day for me is when I sell 25 percent of everything I've got; that's a real good day.

You don't make much money, but it's better than some jobs. And I like being out in the open, by myself, watching the people.

Well, one day a man in his fifties or sixties was slowly walking up the sidewalk to my corner. I noticed him because he was wearing a bright colorful sweater that I couldn't help but see.

It took him a long time to get to my corner. I thought he would just keep walking, but he came right up to me, so I figured he wanted some flowers.

He said, "Young man, I've seen you many times at this spot and I've never seen anyone buy even one flower from you. Well, I'm gonna buy some flowers. How much?"

I told him the price for the daisies and the price for the roses.

"I want daisies and roses," he said, smiling at me sort of funny.

I grabbed one bunch of each. I liked him, so I picked out the best.

"No, no, no!" he said. "I want to buy it all. Every flower you've got."

I couldn't believe it. He took out an old leather wallet and pulled out lots and lots of money. He looked up at me and his smile got real big.

I was so nervous and excited, I didn't really know what to say. I just started trying to figure out how much it would cost to sell all the flowers I had.

I began to gather them together, but then I realized that he couldn't carry them all. But I kept pickin' 'em up.

Then he put his hand on my arm to stop me, and said, "Young man, I'll bet you have a ladyfriend."

I said, "Her name is Ana; she lives on my block."

He said, "Tonight you will arrange your flowers on her doorstep."

He paid me more than the flowers cost and began walking slowly back down the sidewalk the same way he had come.

That was the one and only day I sold a hundred percent of the flowers. It's a day I'll always remember.

I hope that man reads this so Ana and I can say thank you.

Flexible Flyer

Eugene K. Carson • *75* • *Retired*

A few months ago I gathered together my seventy-year-old mind, all its bits and pieces scattered hither and yon, for a small conference. My purpose was to try and recall some of my childhood experiences before Alzheimer's obliterated them from their small storage compartment.

Not that anyone cares about my memories, but maybe some of my pals from yesteryear would like to have their minds jogged back to an era when both mother and father (believe it or not) lived in the same house.

Talking to myself, as old people sometimes do, I said, *I'll write a series of poems about growing up during the depression in a small Midwestern town.*

If wealth is measured by friends and family, then we were by all means wealthy. If wealth is measured monetarily, then we were very poor. The average wage a family of four could get by on was one dollar per day, but you had to be lucky to find work.

My fondest wish in those days was for a new sled, preferably the Cadillac of sleds—the Flexible Flyer, which cost about ten dollars. We could have lived for two weeks on that much money, so I knew I would never have the sled, but "wishes are free and dreams a dime a dozen," Mom would say.

One of the poems I recently wrote describes my wish to go

back to Linn Street hill. The city used to block off the streets just for sliding. As I slid down that hill toward the fairgrounds on my old sled, I made believe it was a Flexible Flyer.

After writing the poem, I wondered if the Flexible Flyer Company was still in business and might enjoy reading it. I checked at a local True Value store and found their address. I sent the poem to Flexible Flyer in West Point, Mississippi.

My mother always said, "There really is a Santa Claus." Once again she was right. On Monday, March 30th, at one o'clock in the afternoon, he was standing at my back door disguised as a United Parcel Service delivery man. He was holding a very large box and had a big smile on his face.

Yes, it was, would you believe?! A Flexible Flyer, with its pretty eagle emblem, arrow and all. My sled had arrived! A childhood Christmas dream, one of those dime-a-dozen, had come true sixty years later.

I can almost hear my mother saying, "See, patience is the virtue of life."

As I sit and admire this long-ago dream, I think of the millions of boys who had wishes like mine. I think of how proud they would have been on Christmas morning to see this beautiful sled under the Christmas tree. How impatient they would have been to rush outside and show off this beauty.

I admire the Flexible Flyer Company, my Earth Angel, and its employees, one and all, for producing a toy that could change the lives of millions of children. There must be a great deal of satisfaction in working for a company such as this.

Thank you, Flexible Flyer, for my Christmas dream. Just as I would have done sixty years ago, my "Flex" is standing at the foot of my bed.

And thanks, Mom. I always believed you.

Flexible Flyer
Things I remember after ages of growing,
How the sledding hills changed without my knowing.
Run and slam make the record go higher,
With the Cadillac of sleds, the Flexible Flyer.
Watch where you slam, or land on your chin,
I still carry scars from way back then.
They blocked the streets for sliding years ago,
Now the chloride and sand make sledding a no-no.
Just one more time lift my spirits up higher,
And give me one more run on my Flexible Flyer.

"A Brief Encounter" by Edith P. Reiss

Michael J. Reiss • 49 • Management Consultant

I am the president of a small community book club, and when I heard about Lorin and Jerry's book, I invited them to speak to our group. In preparation for their visit, I called my mother, who is a writer and storyteller, knowing she would have a story for me to offer.

"Mom, you're full of stories. You've been telling and writing stories all my life. Surely you have one about an Earth Angel."

"Let me think about this," she replied. "Well, I've written seventeen stories, but none of them are really about Earth Angels."

After we concluded our conversation, it suddenly occurred to me that she is an Earth Angel. She was a welfare nurse for the British army during World War II, and the story of her life is the story of an Earth Angel.

I remembered a particular autobiographical piece she wrote called "A Brief Encounter." It tells how my mother, Edith P. Reiss, took a few moments out of a hectic day to help a stranger. Here is her story . . .

It was 1962. I had been visiting family and friends in England for over two weeks, and the following morning I was leaving from Heathrow Airport on a plane to Miami. On this day, I was traveling on an underground train in London. I looked at my watch—almost six o'clock; perhaps I would have time to stop on Oxford Street at Selfridges Department store to buy a small gift for my husband.

Climbing down the stone steps that led to the street, I noticed that it was pouring outside. I put up my umbrella, but just as I got to the last step. there was a heavy gush of wind and the tip of my umbrella hooked onto something. As I pulled, I noticed a tall man looking down on me from the top step. He was attempting to unhook my umbrella from the button of his overcoat. He looked at me with a stern face and two very blue eyes.

"I am so sorry," I said, and moved on down the steps.

I decided to forgo taking the bus. Because of the weather, I may have had to wait some time. I re-entered the London underground, bought another ticket, and waited for the train that would go directly to the Cumberland Hotel, where I would stay the night. Once on the train, I looked for a nonsmoking compartment.

I took a seat and a tall man sat opposite me. He was wearing a felt hat and Burberry-style overcoat, and he stared across at me with his blue eyes. Then I noticed that he was the man I had hooked with my umbrella. He stared at me and, it appeared, through me. He was deep in thought.

At the fourth station, I alighted from the train and entered the Cumberland Hotel. I was at the desk, asking the clerk if there were any messages for me, when I noticed the blue-eyed man standing to my left.

Later, at six-thirty in the evening, I decided to go to the ground floor and have dinner. There was a short line, but the cafeteria seating was somewhat full. I took my tray, and looking around, found a table for two. I proceeded to put down my dishes when I heard a voice say, "May I sit with you?" I looked up and, yes, it was the blue-eyed man.

As I ate, I noticed that he was pushing his food from one side of the plate to the other. I looked at him and commented on what a terrible day it was, with such bad weather.

He put down his knife and fork, pushed his plate away, and said, "Yes, for me it *was* a terrible day, perhaps the worst of my life."

"What makes today so terrible for you?" I asked.

"I feel my life is ended, and I've nothing to live for," he said.

"What happened?" I asked.

He sat silently, and then, looking across at me, said, "My son, our son, killed himself two weeks ago. He was only seventeen."

Here I was, a complete stranger, and he had revealed this to me—it was like a bombshell. I instinctively knew that this man planned to take his own life and that I had to reach within myself to find the words he needed.

"My wife is blaming me for this tragedy," he said.

He went on to tell me that eight months earlier his mother had died of cancer, and that his father had died of a heart attack three months later. Then, just two months ago, his wife had lost her mother in an automobile accident.

Now his son, their only child, was gone.

Since there were no other relatives, he and his wife were trying to cope with all these problems. And now, since his wife had put all the blame on him, he felt that he had nothing to live for.

He put his right hand on the table. I reached out and put my hand over his and gently said, "Let's move to the lobby; it will be more comfortable." We found a corner area and sat down. People were milling around, walking past us, and music was coming from another room. He looked around and motioned for us to move to another, quieter corner.

I wondered how I could possibly give comfort to this distraught man whom I did not know.

He told me he was an engineer and that his job required that he be out of town from time-to-time; his wife had been alone when their son died. I told him that he should immediately go to his wife, hold her tenderly, and tell her that he loved her, assure her and reassure her that he loved her. Both of them should go to their doctor, as neither had been eating or sleeping; he should take time off from his job; stay close to his wife; and try to get some counseling.

I asked if he or his wife were religious.

"No," he told me.

I told him that sometimes a minister could give some comfort and strength at such a crucial time.

I asked him to try to understand that his wife had been angry about all that had happened, and that sometimes we lash out at the ones we love the most. It may have been her way of dealing with this tragedy. We all react in different ways.

Realizing he hadn't introduced himself, he told me that his name was Ernest. Then he continued, "I never told my son that I loved him and now it's too late." His voice trembled.

"Perhaps whenever you visit your son's grave, you can talk to him, talk out loud, and tell him that you love him. Also, tell your wife again and again that you love her. Together, you will pull through this."

I looked at my watch. It was past nine o'clock and I had a very long journey—fourteen hours by prop plane from London to Miami. I realized that I had not told him my name, so I introduced myself.

"Yes, I know," he said. "I saw your name and address on the sticker on your umbrella."

I laughed and told him that I had lost so many umbrellas that I had put a sticker on the handle of this one. We stood up and I noticed tears in his eyes. He bent down, kissed my forehead, and moved away.

That year, at Christmastime, I got many cards from England, and among them was a beautiful one with the words, "Eternally grateful." It was signed Ernest. There was no sender's name or address, just a postmark stamped Birmingham, England.

For the next thirty years, until five years ago, I received a lovely Christmas card, always with meaningful words, and sometimes signed Ernest or Ernie.

Now, I Believe

Sheila Stern • *56* • *Professional Secretary*

I went to the cemetery on the one-year anniversary of my husband's death. My son had planned to meet me because he didn't want me to be alone. I felt extremely depressed and lonely; my husband had been too young to die. He was my best friend and I needed him.

I arrived at the cemetery before my son; this was unusual, since he was always on time. I went to the bench near my husband's resting place and looked down at the headstone. I couldn't hold back the tears, and I began to sob.

When I opened my eyes, someone was standing in front of me. I looked up to see the bright face of a young woman.

"I noticed you sitting here and I wondered if you needed some company," she said in a soft voice.

"No, thank you. My son is meeting me," I replied, wiping my tears.

"Well, could you use a hug?" she asked.

I don't normally hug strangers, but there was something special about this woman. "Yes, that would be nice."

As she hugged me, she whispered in my ear, "He will always be with you."

She walked away and was gone. When my son arrived, he apologized for being late and asked if I was okay.

I told him I was fine, and said, "I have just been hugged by an angel."

I can't even remember what that young woman looked like, but I will never forget her words, which seemed to lift the sadness for the first time. I hope she knows how much her message touched me and lifted my soul. I now believe my husband is with me in some way, and I talk to him often.

Chapter 4

Teachers and Lessons

Thanks, thanks to thee, my worthy friend,
for the lesson thou hast taught!
—*Henry Wadsworth Longfellow*
(from "The Village Blacksmith")

As children, we don't see our teachers as ordinary people. They seem larger than life. When we are older, we realize that they really were larger than life. The valuable gifts teachers give stay with us.

Like the wise old man on the mountaintop, our teachers seem all-knowing and their words of wisdom can be powerful enough to last a lifetime. And, like our parents, they discipline, guide, protect, nurture, influence, and serve as role models. However, while parents are Earth Angels to their own children, teachers can be Earth

Angels to hundreds. From nursery school to college, there are teachers who go above and beyond the curriculum. They have the ability to see past the textbooks and chalkboards and into the eyes of each of their students. This is the quality that makes them Earth Angels.

While searching for stories, it seemed that almost everyone had something to say about a teacher who had made a profound difference in their life. We even heard a story about a very strict teacher who gave a bad grade on a math test. Years later the former student wanted to thank his teacher for the bad grade. He said, "Because she gave me the grade that I deserved, I kept away from math and pursued my more creative side."

A story you will read in this chapter, "Miss Vandemark," shows how deeply a child can be affected by the advice of a teacher. Because of this woman and the care she gives her students, Gerardo, the storyteller, believes that she has prevented many of his classmates from joining gangs. Even though it is years since he has been in her class, she continues to meet once a week with him and his friends just to talk about life.

Though many of the lessons we learn while growing up are taught in the classroom, it is most often outside the classroom that

we are educated about life. Some of the stories in this chapter illus-
trate that you don't have to be a teacher to teach. All of us can be
enlightened by the lessons of others.

The Wonderful World of Fiction

Michael J. Reiss • 49 • Management Consultant

When I was young I had a speech and learning disability. At that time, kids with difficulties such as mine were simply thrown into a lower reading group. There was high, medium, low—and then my group.

My fifth grade teacher, Mr. Marshall, saw that the children in the class would laugh at me and exclude me from many of the activities. So, he went out of his way to make me feel special. He chose me as Projector Monitor, which, in the fifth grade, was a very prestigious honor. This helped raise my self-esteem and it also raised the respect my classmates had for me.

One day Mr. Marshall took me aside and said, "I know you're very smart." Those words meant so much coming from a man who I looked up to. Before then, I had never thought of myself as "smart." After all, I was in the lowest reading group.

My favorite time in class was story time where Mr. Marshall would read and we would sit quietly. I will always remember the day he read the story of a hawk. In the story, you were in the mind of the hawk. I was so intrigued by this, and inspired by the way Mr. Marshall read the words, that I ran to the library and checked out that book. I used my finger to skim along the words and carefully I pronounced each one. It took me two months to get through it.

After that, I checked out the next book in that series, and it took me one month to read. By the time I finished the entire series, I was reading normally and my speech had greatly improved.

In college I began a tutoring service where I helped children with disabilities similar to my own. I became a professional tutor and even went on to get my M.B.A. and Ph.D.

Several years ago I wrote Mr. Marshall a letter saying, "I want to thank you for changing my life."

Because of him, I have been able to help other children, and, about six years ago, I started a Great Books Club where a group of adults gathers monthly to discuss literature. We have read over fifty-two works of fiction, most of which, like *Ulysses, the Iliad*, and *the Odyssey*, are classics.

My Earth Angel, Mr. Marshall, inspired me to find confidence within myself. This confidence, throughout the years, has enabled me to share my love of the written word by bringing others into the wonderful world of fiction.

Like Shakespeare

Carol • *54* • *Teacher*

Sister Paulinus, head of the English department at Marywood College in Scranton, Pennsylvania, taught the advanced composition class. She paused frequently when she spoke, giving her sentences an aura of drama unusual in a lecture to college freshmen.

I was the first in my family to attend college, and I was a little intimidated because most of my classmates had attended exclusive private schools where creative writing and other electives abounded. I, on the other hand, had graduated from a small rural high school where only six or so teachers comprised the entire four-year faculty.

Our first assignment was to write a short story. Sister made very few other specifications, allowing our imaginations free rein. I remember feeling quite proud when I handed in my "masterpiece." It had a boy-meets-girl plot, and I had polished it until I was certain that every word was perfect.

Sister devoted an entire class period to each of our stories, returning them one at a time so that the budding author could read her work to the class and subject it to the reactions of her classmates.

The other girls' stories were marvels—eerie science fiction, humorous bits of whimsy, spine-tingling mysteries. The more I heard, the more I knew how truly ordinary my own pathetic efforts were. I dreaded the day I would have to take my turn before the class.

It was several weeks before Sister Paulinus returned my assignment. With much trepidation, I read my offering aloud. My classmates found even more faults than I had imagined they would! It was "trite," the subject had been "done to death," it was "completely lacking in imagination"—even now, their words ring in my memory. The one-hour ordeal seemed to take days.

Wondering if the barrage would ever end, I heard Sister's leisurely singsong inquiry, "Can't you see what Carol has done? She has taken a very ordinary plot and, by her creative use of words, has made it sparkle like new. Shakespeare often did the very same thing."

I couldn't believe my ears! Despite the flaws, Sister had not only found something in my work worth praising, but had compared it to Shakespeare's. I floated out of class that day.

Years have passed, and I never did tell Sister Paulinus how much her praise meant to my adolescent ego. Like Sister Paulinus, I became a teacher. My heart always goes out to the faltering student, and I make a point of speaking a few words of encouragement. I often wonder if Sister Paulinus, my Earth Angel, had any inkling of how many generations of students she would transform the day she spoke those words of hope to one insecure young woman so many years ago.

Coach Johnson

Tod Anthony Eggimann • *16* • *Goal: Professional Baseball Player*

When I was in the fifth grade, I wanted nothing more than to play professional baseball. The only problem: I considered myself a terrible baseball player; I couldn't hit or throw as well as I wanted.

Then a coach, a very special coach, came into my life. His name was Nat Johnson.

When I tried out for Little League, he picked me up because he said I showed tons of potential. After practice every day he stayed on the field with me and worked on my swing, my batting stance, and my throwing form. No other coach had ever gone out of his way for me.

I began to develop a friendship with him. Coach Johnson wasn't just doing his job; he cared about my dreams and went the extra mile to help me make them come true.

As the weeks went by, my skills progressed, and my name started showing up in the Little League newspaper. By the time the season was nearly half over, I had worked my way up to where I wanted to be—lead-off batter, starting center fielder, and a rocket throw from center field to home plate.

My dream was becoming a reality, and the highlight of my season came when I was chosen to play on the Thousand Oaks Little League World Series team.

From that moment, I knew that one day the announcer would call my name, and I would trot out to center field to play in my first game at a major-league stadium. When that happens, I plan to dedicate the moment to Nat Johnson, my coach, my friend, my Earth Angel.

Miss Vandemark

Gerardo M. Gonzalez • *14* • *Goal: Veterinarian*

I remember the day I started fourth grade; I thought that I was bigger and tougher than anyone else. That day, my friends and I were waiting to see our new teacher. When we heard the bell, we all lined up. We were talking and laughing when a young woman came up to us and said, "Good morning, kids, I am your teacher this year."

We all stood there with astonished looks on our faces. Then we looked around at each other. The boys were like, "Do you see how pretty she is?"

You know how women react to things like that, so the teacher just said, "Go into the classroom," in a very serious voice.

Once we were in our seats, she took the roll and said, "Hi, my name is Miss Vandemark. Can you say my name?"

We tried to pronounce her name but couldn't.

Again, a little slower, she said, "Miss V-a-n-d-e-m-a-r-k."

The class tried again.

Then Miss Vandemark showed us what we were going to do with the little book she handed out. It was yellowish, and it was called a journal. Miss Vandemark told us that every day we would write a page of answers to questions she put on the board. For example, "Do you like this classroom? Why?"

The first day of school, Miss Vandemark was all right. The second day, she gave us a lot of homework. When I got home I showed my mom how much she had given us and my mom said, "Well, you'd better start right now."

So I did, and I didn't finish until 11:30 at night!

The next day, when some kids didn't do their homework, we got to know Miss Vandemark better. She was really mean, and she started yelling and screaming at those poor guys who didn't finish their homework.

Who would have thought she was yelling at us so we would be good, hard-working students and do our homework? I guess, because we were little kids, we didn't know that she was trying to make sure we would work hard so we could be somebody.

By the end of fourth grade, we all loved Miss Vandemark, and she loved us too. She still yelled at us, but not as much and not as badly.

When fourth grade was over, we were very sad because we were going to have to leave Miss Vandemark to go on to the fifth grade where we were supposed to have a new teacher who didn't even give homework. How was I supposed to learn that way?

Well, we talked to Miss Vandemark; some of us were crying. She was crying too, and she said that she would talk with the principal to see if she could trade places with the fifth grade teacher. The bell rang, and we left class thinking about what she had said.

When I got home, I sat at the dining room table and did my homework. We had math and reading, and we had to write twenty spelling words twenty times each. I took a shower and went to bed.

The next morning, when I woke up, I couldn't help worrying that I would have to leave this teacher who had taught me so much. I finally got up and rode my bike to school. When I realized the bell had already rung, I ran to class. When I walked in, Miss Vandemark had a smile on her face.

She said, "Good morning, everyone. I have some good news for you. I spoke with Miss Perez and she said that I may teach fifth grade. So, you all will be with me next year."

We were very excited.

In the fifth grade Miss Vandemark gave us a lot of good advice. She talked to us about gangs. She said they were not good for us and, if we needed somebody to talk to, we could always find a family member or someone in school. She said, "You don't need to join gangs. A lot of bad things happen in gangs and out in the streets, so be careful. I don't want to read about you in the newspaper someday." She told us it would hurt her deeply if anything bad ever happened to any of us.

She was more than just a teacher; other teachers just teach, they don't talk about real life. She taught us what to do and what not to do and this was really important during that time in our lives. She also talked to us for hours about college and getting a great job and career so we would be useful in life.

Even though I am now in the eighth grade, I visit her every Thursday. She takes the time to sit with me and my friends and helps us with things we need to talk about. No other teacher I have ever had has done that. She loves us.

No doubt about it, Miss Vandemark is my Earth Angel. If I hadn't met her, my life would have been very different. Because of her, I think about my future; I am planning to become a veterinarian. The day I graduate from college, I will be thinking of Miss Vandemark; I will never forget her.

Mr. Dillon

Linda Slater • 52 • Psychotherapist

I was fourteen and sliding my way through the school year, doing as little as possible and getting Bs and Cs. (I don't remember when I started getting bored, though in the third grade I began staring out the window of the little school, watching the light as it fell on the leaves of the cottonwoods.)

Tall and smart, I was usually placed in the back of the room. The teacher knew I knew the answers and didn't call on me often. I would put a library book behind the assigned one and read about Robin Hood and Nancy Drew and the Box Car family. I dreamed of living in a box car, leaving that small town, and going to exotic places.

One day Mr. Dillon, the school principal, pulled me out of class and took me to the teacher's lounge to talk. He was like a little gnome, I had always thought, with his short stature, his large funny nose, his larger head, and his thick glasses.

"It's time to think about your future," he started. "Do you know that you could be somebody—a leader maybe, if you tried harder? And this world and this school need more leaders."

He stopped to see my reaction and, frankly, I was stunned. No one had ever talked to me like this before.

"I want you to go home tonight and decide: do you want to

be average, or do you want to start achieving and become a leader? We'll talk again tomorrow afternoon."

That night I thought about many things, and I decided to wake up, work harder, and do more than just get by.

Mr. Dillon took me under his wing and treated me like an adult. We met in the teacher's lounge about once a week from then on. This Earth Angel of mine performed a very important intervention. He made me see that anyone could be average, but that I had the potential to be special and do great things.

Because of Mr. Dillon, I ran for class president that year and won. The next year I got into the Honor Society, and later became student body president and won several scholarships to college.

Even today, when I catch myself staring out a window, I think of Mr. Dillon and pick myself up again.

Follow the Rule

Cindee Geyer • 36 • Substance Abuse Counselor

Three years ago my whole world changed. I was fighting alcoholism, a very difficult drug addiction, and a deep depression.

I had never fit in: not in my family, not at school, never at a party unless I had a few beers to take the edge off, not at work, not at my father's funeral, not even in my own skin. I was in the greased barrel with no way out. With my self-esteem and self-confidence at an all-time low I had to do something. My two daughters were depending on me and, if I couldn't do it for myself, I had to do it for them. I felt so alone; I had alienated everyone.

My entire life had been a facade. I had not been sober one day in fifteen years. I had built my world around alcohol. I had found a job that I could do at home so I could be with my girls, I told myself, as they were growing up. In actuality, it was so I could maintain my blood alcohol level. As a single mother, I had accomplished a lot; six months pregnant, I had moved to California from Virginia with an eight-month-old baby. I did it all by myself. In two years I had bought a house by myself. These things kept people from seeing the person I really was—I was sick every morning, sipped beer all day, and I couldn't cook dinner unless I had a drink within reach. This continued for many years.

I finally went to see a doctor because I was so depressed. He gave me Valium to help. When it wasn't enough, I called him and he increased the dosage.

My isolated world came crashing in on me when, one day, the pills and alcohol caused an accidental overdose. I was taken to the hospital by ambulance, unconscious and not breathing. When I woke up in the Intensive Care Unit, I wished I had not woken up at all. My seventeen-year-old daughter was standing there screaming, "How can you do this to me!"

When I returned from the hospital, I looked at my girls and realized it was time to do something.

First I got rid of the pills. I remember thinking, *There are going to be some very happy fish out there*, as I flushed 120 Valium down the toilet. After calling the pharmacy to tell them not to refill any more prescriptions, no matter what, I settled in to detoxify myself. After three days of shaking and sweating and muscle cramps, I could barely function. I knew I needed help. At thirty-four, I had to learn how to walk, talk, think, and drive—sober.

I headed out to find one of "those" meetings. I had a preconceived idea that the people at Alcoholics Anonymous were just a bunch of old men with red swollen noses and gravelly voices who sat around and talked about the good ol' days of drinking. Nevertheless, I needed help and it seemed that I had nowhere else to go.

At my first meeting, there were only six people, but I was frightened to death. A few fit my stereotype of an alcoholic, but, for the most part, the people were young and had bright eyes. They were laughing and had a wonderful warm glow. They asked if anyone in their first thirty days of sobriety would like to introduce themselves so others could get to know them.

Wait, let's get this straight. They wanted *me* to say my name, and that "I'm an alcoholic!?" Absolutely not! I was not going to fall for that setup. I didn't talk to anyone, and no one talked to me.

I had been running a day care in my home for years, so I had been able to isolate myself from adults. I only left the house if I needed to go to the grocery store. I don't remember this, but my nineteen-year-old daughter tells me that when she was fifteen, I would hand her the keys to the car and tell her to go to the market for me. I was very fearful of people and learning to interact with strangers had been hard enough loaded. How would I do it sober?

After going to these meetings a few days in a row—and still not talking to anyone—one of the men came up to me. The first things I noticed about him were his soft blue eyes and strong arms. He saw that I was scared and unsure, but he approached me anyway. He put his arm around me and said, "It's going to be all right." With those words, I broke down and cried. I'm not sure why, but I cried and cried. It was what I needed, desperately. I felt such a wonderful comfort from this man, and I knew instantly that I could trust him.

Larry was there every night, and every night he gave me a hug, and every night I cried. I needed someone who was not judgmental and who was genuine. I had a lot of difficult things to face—I was feeling weak and fragile, and I needed some gentle support. I also needed to talk things out with someone who understood what I was going through. I really needed to talk to my father, but he was dead. In place of him, it seemed God had put someone in my life who understood me better than I understood myself. Although he was not old enough to be a father figure, there was something comforting and nonthreatening about him. He was sincere and he helped me in a gentle way. He was what I needed to be eased into the sober society gently and slowly.

Because of Larry, the barriers I had built began to crumble. He even told me once, "I know that you have a wall of protection, but whenever I hug you, I can feel a brick come out of that wall."

I had been ready to surrender my life. I just needed an Earth Angel to guide me in the right direction. I needed someone to show me that there are people in this world who could love me for me. Without realizing it, this gentle man taught a stubborn woman that the real world could be a safe and beautiful place. The gifts Larry gave me were trust, faith, and the pathways that led me to a better life. If it hadn't been for Larry, I wouldn't have been so open to meeting my fiancé, Greg, and allowing myself to be loved.

After a few weeks, Larry told me it was a rule that I had to hug him before I left each night. We laughed. I remember several times being in the car on the way home after a meeting and suddenly realizing that I'd forgotten to hug him. No matter how far away I had gone, I always turned the car around, ran back in, and gave him our hug.

To this day, almost two years later, I'm still sober and I still follow that rule. I am now a substance abuse counselor for people convicted of driving under the influence of alcohol.

I want to thank my Earth Angel for saving my life. He was the only one at those meetings with the courage to walk up to someone so closed. Because he went out of his way to get through to me, I stayed at those meetings and was able to change my life.

Larry's hugs have filled my world with warmth, security, and love. Now, whenever I hug someone else, I feel like I am passing along Larry's gift.

The Busboy

Marcell Patrick Brickey • *24* • *Junior High School Teacher*

As a fourteen-year-old busboy, I saw the world with the eyes of a manual laborer. While keenly aware of the minor role my presence played in the mornings of tourists and traveling salesmen, I considered myself a sort of litmus test to the customers I served. If they were rude or condescending, they must be bad people.

The restaurant I worked in was in a large motel in the Pocono Mountains of Pennsylvania. Most of our customers were tourists from New York or business folk passing through. As a busboy, my main job was to keep their coffee cups full and get their dirty plates out of sight as soon as possible.

The weekends were the toughest days to work, as the crowds lined up outside the door and the tables were occupied before I could completely reset them. Toward the end of a weekend morning, my nerves were usually frayed and my legs very tired.

The sight of a group of six people was anything but welcome, but this is what I faced the morning I would meet my Earth Angel.

They stood at the door in their Sunday finest, dresses and suits with faces on top. I didn't feel like looking into their eyes as I set down fork, knife, and spoon, and headed wearily to the menu rack.

"Good morning, table for six?" I asked.

Silence. Awkward silence.

"Table for six?" I was nearly yelling. "Would you like a table for six people?"

"Um . . . yes . . . that would be fine." The lady's voice was quiet but firm, as if she were attempting not to be heard by anyone.

I led them to their table and was careful to pull the chairs out for the three ladies in the party. Not one of them thanked me for this act of chivalry, and I had already written them off as rude and worthy of contempt.

I headed back to the kitchen to summon the waitress and fetch a pot of coffee. Their breakfast was quiet and deliberate. They seemed to say as little to each other as they did to me, flagging me down occasionally to request another refill on their coffee.

My already-worn patience was further dissipated when one of the gentlemen in the party asked me where the restrooms were. I directed him to the lobby and soon followed, as nature was calling.

He was smoking a cigarette when I walked in, and he seemed glad to see me.

"We must be pretty tough people to wait on," he said with half a smile.

"It's okay, it's my job to be nice to you."

He smiled again, just before he changed the way I looked at my world.

"My mother died two days ago and my family just got back from her funeral. It was a rather sudden death and it's been a very difficult weekend for all of us."

I froze as I was pulling my hands from the sink. I stared at the mirror where I could see him standing behind me. "I'm so sorry" were the only words I managed to get out.

"It's all right, you had no way of knowing and I probably should have said something on the way in. Thanks for your condolences."

He handed me a five-dollar bill and left me standing there, my perspective completely turned around. It was a lesson from a stranger about judging people; a lesson about kindness and understanding.

I think back to this incident whenever I catch myself rushing to judge someone whose first impression hasn't been a good one. I haven't a clue what that gentleman's name was nor do I think that he would remember me. But I will always remember him as an Earth Angel sent to teach me the importance of taking an extra moment to look a little deeper.

Randy

Carol Hatcher • 50 • Copy Editor

The first time I saw Randy I was horrified. His advertisement said he was disabled, but it had in no way prepared me for what I saw.

His mother met me at the door in a blue Hawaiian-print shirt. She was a large, matter-of-fact woman with a laugh in her voice that took the edge off the situation. She led me to a family room warmed by the fire in the woodstove. The fragrance of alder smoke mixed with that of fall apples.

Randy was lying on a huge colonial-style couch. His mother

pulled a rocker close to the couch and told me to make myself at home. The chair was closer than I was comfortable with, but I didn't want to seem rude by moving it. Reluctantly I sat down, committed to looking at the frail twisted body on the couch. I suppressed the cowardly urge to run back to my car and drive home, pretending I'd never seen the ad requesting help for a disabled writer.

Randy's body was no more than a skeleton, the skin stretched over the bones. He was dressed in blue cotton pants, a red flannel shirt, and sneakers that bore signatures and drawings put there by friends.

The size of his body was that of a ten-year-old, but I could see ageless wisdom and humor in his eyes. At twenty-four, he looked as if he had discovered the secrets of the universe.

When Randy spoke, I understood why the chair had been placed so close to the couch. His chest heaved with the effort and the result was barely audible. His jaw was rigid and his teeth too large for the shrunken face, making it difficult for him to speak clearly. I didn't understand the first ten sentences and began to panic. How would I sound like an intelligent applicant when I couldn't even understand his questions? But, as if familiar with my dilemma, he kept talking until I became accustomed to his speech and he could see that I was understanding him.

We talked for over two hours. The questions were not what I expected in a job interview. Who is my favorite author and why? What are my religious beliefs and what, if any, type of prayer do I engage in? What family activities do I enjoy? The questions were personal, but I wasn't offended. By the end of the interview I felt as if I'd known Randy for centuries.

I was hired. From one o'clock until four on Mondays, Wednesdays, and Fridays, I went to the comfortable room where the stillness was barely disturbed by the voice of the old young man who called himself a Buddha. We talked openly and casually about life and death, as if they were the same, and I came to see it that way. At an early age Randy had learned to live with the knowledge that death was close and could come in the form of a common cold brought home by one of his brothers. On several occasions his parents were told that the end was imminent. He told me of the dreams he'd had at those times that a beautiful lady in white had come for him, but that he had asked her to wait. He said that in daylight he could talk about death as if he were discussing his evening meal: "I'm going to die; so what, I'm going to die." But in the middle of the night he would awaken in a cold sweat screaming, "My God, I'm going to die!"

Some days we spent the entire three hours talking about my life: how my son was adjusting to kindergarten, my husband's work, how I felt when my cat died. At first I felt that I was cheating Randy out of his writing time by talking about myself. But he asked probing questions, never satisfied with a brief or shallow answer, and I came to understand that this was the only way for him to know about life beyond his room. He often began sessions by saying, "Ask me a question." When I drew blanks, he questioned me.

There were days when Randy would lighten things up with his impressions of W. C. Fields and Groucho Marx. Eventually, trying not to laugh, I would get us back on track and we'd write a beautiful poem.

Intimacy grew between us, almost unnoticed by me and in spite of my conscious effort not to become close. Randy had already outlived all medical predictions and I knew our time could be short. But Randy's need for honesty transcended any need I had to protect my vulnerability.

Writing was the driving force in his life. Denied the use of his hands, he had to depend on someone else. That level of exposure required mutual understanding, respect, and trust.

Before he died, Randy wrote his own eulogy. In it he said:

"If I speak in high praise of myself, it is with the knowledge that my life has been blessed with friends and family who also deserve high praise. I know that I shall continue beyond my death, and that the love I have with those close to me shall also continue and deepen; I love you. We are never apart."

I had nine years with Randy, an Earth Angel through and through. I didn't work for him all that time, but we remained close friends, and he always helped me put the important aspects of my life in focus. When my baby daughter was born critically ill, he kept in close phone contact with me, telling me never to give up on her. When I was considering divorce, he asked me pointed questions about what I needed in a relationship, and he forced me to see for myself what I was not getting from my marriage.

Knowing Randy taught me to keep my life in perspective and to always be aware of the bigger scheme.

Staring Down the Leopard

Bonita Evans, Ph.D. • 57 • Youth Advocate

Over the years, I have come to believe that we often live in fear of circumstances and situations that rarely come to pass. We tend to become victims of anticipated outcomes. While it is true that there are consequences to everything we do, we must learn how to "stare down the leopard."

You are probably asking yourself what that means. Well, it is a piece of advice I was given shortly before I had one of the most frightening experiences of my life.

In the early 1960s, I saw an advertisement in the *New York Times* that offered employment to anyone who could use a court reporter's machine and was willing to move to Africa for two years to work in the Kenyan Parliament. At the time, I had no idea what the machine looked like or how it was operated, other than what I had seen on "Perry Mason." But, I wanted to go to Africa, and I was very willing to let someone else pay my way. I answered the ad, enrolled in a stenotyping school, and, in a short time, I had earned my certificate.

January was a perfect time to arrive in Kenya; it was the middle of the dry season, and the weather was glorious. Good weather, it seemed, signaled the need for residents of this country to visit safari parks. During the first few months of my stay, every weekend seemed taken up with watching animals. I, however, have always felt that if you've seen one lion, you've seen them all.

Many times during my first year in Kenya, it was a source of embarrassment to me that I was unable to see an animal in the wild unless it was standing in the open; this was a source of amusement for my Kenyan friends. It also didn't help my reputation that I screamed at the sight of any large insect.

Then the servant of a friend took the time to tell me many interesting things about animals, and, by this act, he became my Earth Angel. One day, as I was driving, I spotted him on the road to Machakos. I offered him a lift, and in return, he told me about the animals. He explained that I shouldn't be ashamed of not being able to see animals in the wild, but that many people, even Africans, had been killed by coming too close to an animal they had not seen.

"If you see a lion or a leopard, you must stand still. They are like kittens. If you have a piece of string on the floor, the cat will pass it and not bother it, but if you pull it while he is looking at it, he will pounce on it. Lions and leopards are the same. If you see one, you must stand still and stare it down. And try not to be afraid, because when humans sweat, the animals can smell that and they will attack. They know that the most dangerous animal in the world is the human being because he has guns."

The next morning, I stood in front of my porch watching the sunrise. Suddenly everything became deathly quiet. Even the leaves on the trees seemed to move in silence, as though they were afraid that the sound would betray their location. I looked to the left—nothing. To the right—nothing. My eyes scanned the area directly in front of me—nothing. When I had begun to think that the whole thing was just in my imagination, I heard the crack of a twig to my left. I looked in its direction and saw two gold eyes looking at me from between the leaves of a bush.

Stand perfectly still. Try not to show fear. Just keep staring at the leopard. The words came into my mind as though the servant was standing beside me. *Keep thinking these thoughts: I'm looking at you, you're looking at me. I don't want to hurt you, and you don't want to hurt me.*

I kept repeating the words over and over, as the leopard left the cover of the bush. He crossed my front lawn within ten yards of me. As he crossed, he kept his eyes on me, and I kept mine on him. We were locked in a silent pact, until he crossed the lawn and disappeared into the bush on the other side.

Since that time—and my two-year experience turned into a

treasured ten—I have not been afraid of much, and though not everyone will encounter a leopard in life, fear can come in many forms. I have come to think of challenges in my life as leopards, and I always remember my Earth Angel's words:

"You must stand still and stare it down."

Chapter 5

Healing Body and Soul

We are each of us
angels with only one wing.
And we can only fly
embracing each other.

—*Luciano de Crescenzo*

The stories in this chapter show that sometimes people need the support of another, whether physically or emotionally, to help them heal. Their Earth Angels appeared at the time they were needed most.

During our search, we met a woman who told us that, when she was a young girl in England, she was confined to a wheelchair, until her Earth Angel appeared from out of nowhere and inspired her to try to walk again.

A young man, who offered to take a picture for us at Ghirardelli Square in San Francisco, shared his story over a hot fudge sundae. He told us how he hadn't been able to reveal a dark secret to his family, until a woman entered his life and led him home.

One Saturday in June, we decided to go to Disneyland. It was a beautiful day and we wanted to be in a place built upon the spirit of goodness.

We had been walking around for a while so we decided to get a cold drink and sit down for a few minutes. We bought some lemonade and looked for a place to sit. The only available seats were at a table already occupied by a man in his thirties, so we asked if we could join him.

"Oh, be my guest," he said, as he pulled out a chair. Then he added, "I'm just waiting for my sister and our friend to come back from Star Tours."

We thanked him and sat down.

After a short silence, the man said, "My name's Joe."

We introduced ourselves and began to talk.

Our conversation turned to what we all did for a living. We told Joe about our book. He was genuinely interested and told us he

thought he might have a story for us. Unprepared, we scrambled for
some Disneyland napkins to write on.

"This happened when I was five years old. Is that okay?" Joe
asked.

We told him it was fine and encouraged him to continue.

About twenty minutes later, as Joe reached the end of his story,
two women approached.

"Sorry for making you wait, Joe," one of the women said. "The
line was longer than we thought."

"Oh, that's okay," he said, as he stood up. Then he turned to
us. "I was just talking with Lorin and Jerry. This is my sister,
Vicky, and this is Shelly."

We shook hands and thanked Joe for sharing his story with us.
We told the women that we felt like we already knew them.

Vicky and Shelly gave Joe a strange look. "I'll tell you all about
it later," he said. Joe turned back toward us, extended his hand,
and said, "Good luck with your search for more Earth Angels."

We talked about Joe all the way home.

Foster

Joe • *30* • *Reporter*

When I was five years old a judge told my mother that, until she stopped drinking and neglecting us, my sister and I would be placed in foster care.

I remember being very frightened. Although my sister, Vicky (who was only two at the time), and I hardly ever saw our mother, that life was all we knew. Who would we live with? Would they be kind to us? Would my sister and I be separated?

We were taken to a shelter. I blocked most of that experience out of my mind, but one day is etched in my memory: the day they came to take my sister out of the shelter and to a foster home—leaving me behind. We clung to each other as long as we could, and we cried.

I was her big brother, and I felt it was my responsibility to take care of her. I didn't talk for a while after that; I just held onto an old blanket I had taken from our home. One of my foster mothers tried to wash it one day, and I remember screaming and holding onto it as tightly as I could. The next day, I was sent back to the shelter.

After that, I was tossed around from home to home. I missed my little sister terribly and I had never felt so lonely.

One day a woman I had never seen walked into the shelter.

She seemed younger than most of the foster mothers I had met. She looked right at me, smiled, and sat down on the bed by my side.

"Hi, Joe, my name is Shelly." Her voice was soft and gentle. "I was thinking that you might like to come live with me, but I'd like you to decide for yourself. Would it be okay if we went to my house for a few days to see how you like it?"

This was the first time anyone had asked me if I *wanted* to go with them.

I had nowhere else to go. And, besides, this rotten kid, Victor, kept trying to take my blanket away. He was such a bully. With Victor's face in mind, I nodded my head.

We were in Shelly's car when she said, "We just have to make one quick stop." She pulled her car into the driveway of an apartment building, and I couldn't believe what I saw next— it was my sister running toward the car.

"Vicky!" I screamed.

Shelly opened the car door for me and I jumped out. Vicky and I ran toward each other. I recall holding her so tightly that she had to push me off. Then we hugged again. I whispered in her ear and promised, "I won't let anyone separate us again." I took Vicky's hand and I was not going to let go. I wasn't going to let this woman take me without my sister.

Shelly smiled at us and said, "I thought a brother and sister should grow up together. What do you say we go get some ice cream and you both come to my house and live with me for a while?"

I was so happy to be with my sister, I didn't care where we were going.

We walked into Shelly's apartment and she told us to follow her. She opened the door to a room that was all ready for us. It had two beds and a large window. Over one bed was a wooden plaque with my name and over the other a wooden flower with the letters of Vicky's name in its petals.

Vicky took to Shelly quickly. She wasn't as afraid to become attached as I was. I watched Shelly and Vicky holding hands and laughing. They had a game where they tickled each other and tried not to laugh.

Shelly read to us every night. One night, a night I will never forget, she handed me three books and asked me which one I wanted her to read. I looked into her eyes, and then I slowly pointed to the book with the dog on the front. It was called, *Are You My Mother?* by P. D. Eastman.

As she read, I began to cry.

She held me and talked to me. It was the first time, since we had left my mother, that I really felt loved.

After that night, Shelly and I became close. I joined the tickling game, and I even agreed to let her wash my blanket. She let me sit on the washing machine and watch through the window of the dryer until it was finished.

Shelly was only twenty-four years old, and unmarried; later I found out that she had put her career on hold so she could take an extra job to help support us.

Vicky and I stayed with Shelly for five years. Each day she told us how happy she was that we were with her. When we were bad, she disciplined us, and when we all cooled off, she reminded us how much she loved us. She promised that, until my mom returned, she would do everything in her power to keep us safe. After being tossed around from one place to another, it felt so comforting to hear that word—*safe*.

Five years later our mother came back for us. I'll never forget that day because it was one of the most difficult of my life. We didn't want to leave Shelly, but we wanted to be with our mother. Though we hardly knew her, we knew we belonged with her. What made it even more difficult was that we were moving to a different state, which, when you are ten years old, may as well be another planet. Shelly, Vicky, and I all hugged and cried. My mother started to cry and hugged Shelly. I'm sure she thanked her.

After a long plane ride we arrived at this strange home and began to unpack.

"Look!" Vicky yelled. "My flower!"

Shelly had secretly wrapped the plaque and flower from above our beds and put them in our suitcases. We hung them above the beds in our new home where they stayed until we moved out.

Soon after we arrived, my mom married a nice man. He adopted us and has been the closest thing we've known to a father.

My mother had a job teaching preschool and she never had another drink. She also never left us alone again. Even today she makes me call her to let her know I'm safe.

It has been twenty years since we left Shelly's, but we have kept in touch through letters, phone calls, e-mail, and occasional trips to California. A couple of times, she has come to Minneapolis to visit us. We consider her part of our family.

I believe those five years in Shelly's care changed me in a way that will stay with me throughout my life. I have tried to thank her in different ways, but how do you thank an angel? Maybe by having children and taking care of them the way Shelly took care of us.

Vicky and I have often talked about adopting children someday when we each get married and have families of our own.

I just want to say, thank you for my life, Shelly, and for being our Earth Angel. When children are in a safe place, with someone who loves them, it can feel like heaven.

The Nice Man

Stacy • 24 • Social Worker for Children

As an infant, I was diagnosed as being partially deaf; however, my type of deafness was considered somewhat correctable. When I was seven years old, I was scheduled to have my first ear surgery at St. Vincent Hospital in Los Angeles. I was very nervous.

The morning of the surgery, I awoke in my hospital room to find myself alone. My mother was staying at a hotel nearby and had not yet arrived to be with me. It was very early, and there didn't seem to be anyone around. I didn't even see any nurses at the nurses' station. As the minutes passed, I grew more frightened and lonely. I started to softly cry.

Suddenly I looked up and saw a big man standing in the doorway of my room. He was larger than life, wearing a beret and a concerned expression.

"Why are you crying?" the big man asked in his deep voice.

"I'm scared," I said.

"Don't cry," he said. He came over and kneeled down to my level. "Watch this . . ." He proceeded to put his fingers in his mouth and blow his cheeks up like balloons! I thought his face would explode! Then he wiggled his ears.

I'd never seen anything like it. I forgot all my worries, and laughed and laughed. Then the nice man said, "Don't be scared. Everything will be all right."

Well, after that, I could hardly think of anything besides his big cheeks and wiggly ears. When my mom arrived, I told her all about the big man who had made me laugh.

As the years passed, I had other ear surgeries and often thought of that big, sweet man who had taken the time to calm the fears of a frightened little girl. I wondered who he was and wished I could somehow thank him. After all, he was my Earth Angel.

Then, one day, my roommate and I were watching the news on television, and a familiar face appeared on the screen. I also recognized the distinctive, deep voice.

"That's him!" I cried. "That's the man who visited me in the hospital when I was little."

We listened in stunned silence as the reporter said that jazz great Dizzy Gillespie had died.

Blue Poppies of Tibet

Pauline Innis • Naturalist

I was just six years old and I knew I looked dreadful. I'd had polio and meningitis, which left me unable to walk; my head was bent to one side, and my right hand and arm were useless. Children ignored me or stood and stared and asked why I was in "that thing." Grown-ups looked at me and then very quickly looked away.

Because noise made my head ache, I was often taken in a push chair to stay with Gertrude Fyleman. She designed children's clothes in her little studio in the quiet seclusion of the Barton Plant Nurseries in Torbay, England.

One day a man came to see Miss Fyleman. I thought he worked in the garden. I had no idea that he was the one who had brought most of the beautiful plants and flowers to the garden from all over the world. It wasn't until much later that I learned he was the famous explorer, Captain Kingdon Ward.

Looking at me, he asked Miss Fyleman, "Who is this young lady?"

"This is Pauline. She comes to keep me company."

"Oh, she must be the young lady you told me about." Then he said, "Would you like to go around the world with me and see the flowers and trees that grow there?"

"Oh, yes. Can we go now?" I couldn't believe that anyone would want to take me anywhere.

"All right, I'll tell you what we'll do," and he reached into the bundle of papers he was carrying. "I'll push you around and you can hold this map, and when I show you the plants, we'll find their country on it so you can see where they came from."

This was how I started the most important journey of my life. As the captain pushed me around, he stopped and pointed to a flower or a tree.

"This is the tree peony from China. That pine tree is from Japan. Now let's look at the map. See, there's China, and Japan is just a bit further south. Can you see those lovely flowers in the pond over there? Those are lotus flowers from Kashmir." And so we studied the map together.

Then I saw something I would never forget. "What are those pretty flowers over there?" I asked, pointing to some deep blue flowers that I thought were more beautiful than any of the others.

"Those? They are the blue poppies of Tibet."

"But poppies are red," I objected.

"Yes, most poppies are red, but there are blue ones in Tibet."

"Where is Tibet? Is it a long way?"

"Yes, it's a very long way. Look, here it is on the map. It's between China and India high up in the Himalayas, the highest mountains in the world."

"I would like to go there and see those pretty flowers."

"Well, perhaps you will one day."

I looked across at the gates that led to the open road. "Would that road take me there?"

"Oh, yes," he answered. "Nowadays you can take that road to the airport and fly there."

"If a person could walk, that road would take them to lots of places, wouldn't it?" I asked wistfully.

For a moment there was no answer. Then the captain said, "You really want to go and see those flowers growing, don't you?"

"Yes, more than anything in the world."

"Well, Miss Fyleman tells me you won't do your exercises anymore, and you won't go to the therapist. Is that true?"

I hung my head lower. "Yes," I whispered. "It hurts to do those things and my hand and legs won't move anyway."

"Well, young lady, if you try very hard and do everything your doctors tell you, you will be able to walk again and go anywhere you like."

"Will I really? Truly?"

"I'm sure of it. If anyone puts their mind to something, they can do wonders."

Well, time passed, and, although I didn't see the captain again, I remembered and believed everything he told me. I struggled every day with the exercises, and I imagined I was in Tibet climbing the great, high mountains covered with beautiful, blue flowers. I loved saying the word *Himalayas*, a wonderful word for a child as it rolls off the tongue with a very important sound.

When the doctors and therapist saw that I was trying to make progress, they renewed their efforts. When you have polio and meningitis, you take on a fetal position. Your legs have to be pulled down straight to exercise the muscles, and it is extremely painful. When I began to walk, I could only walk on my toes and I needed much assistance.

But I didn't want to be an invalid anymore. I wanted to be able to travel the world, just like the captain. I was very lucky to have met him when I did. And as it turned out, fighting the illness gave me the courage to eventually do a lot of things few women did—like crossing the Indies on a mule.

We moved away from Torbay and the blue poppies, but they stayed in my mind with other childhood memories, like tea on the beach with Devonshire cream and fancycakes.

As time passed, though, I wondered whether blue poppies really existed or whether it was just a child's imagination. I saw all kinds of poppies—red, white, pink, and yellow, but never blue.

When I was in my twenties, I went back to Torbay to look for them, but alas, houses had been built where the nurseries used to be, and no one seemed to remember them.

So the poppies remained a mystery until one night. I was a member of the International Society of Women Geographers; since women were not allowed to join the Explorers Club, they had begun a club of their own. (Margaret Mead and Amelia

Earhart were also members.) The men of the Explorers Club generously invited the women of our club to a reception for the brother of the Dalai Lama. The hostess asked me to make a cup of tea for him, as he did not drink alcohol, and I was delighted to do so for such a distinguished person.

After I poured the tea, he invited me to sit down beside him. Suddenly I realized that this was my opportunity to really find out about the blue poppies. Dare I ask? Suppose they only existed in my imagination?

But the monk looked so kind that I said, "Do you mind if I ask a question about Tibet?"

"I would be most pleased."

And so I told him about Captain Kingdon Ward and the blue poppies, and I asked him if they really grow in the mountains of Tibet.

"They are the most beautiful sight in the world. We call them the flowers of heaven, because they reflect the blue of the sky. Against the snow they are an unforgettable vision. One day I hope you go and see them for yourself."

I almost had my chance five years ago, when I was invited to a wedding in Tibet. I was awaiting a telephone call from Tibet to arrange my travels. When the phone rang, I ran to answer it, and in my excitement, I fell and broke my ankle. It would have been a difficult journey, and I couldn't have made it in that condition.

One day I hope to get there and see the blue poppies growing—even just a little glimpse. I often wonder if the flowers are as beautiful as I remember; or perhaps they are so beautiful because they bring back my memories of the captain.

Captain Kingdon Ward died in 1959 having made twenty-two expeditions in search of flowers and trees. He received the George White Medal from the Massachusetts Horticultural Society and the Forbes Medal from the Royal Geographers Society.

I didn't realize, until I was older, how much he helped me. Isn't it wonderful that such a famous man bothered with a sickly child? It was so very kind.

I wish, so much, that I had had the opportunity to thank this great man, my Earth Angel, for taking the time to show me the world and its treasures and inspiring me to learn to walk. Because of his encouragement, I was given a second chance and have had a most fulfilling life.

Captain Kingdon Ward will always live in my grateful memory among the flowers of heaven.

And Smiles to Go Before I Sleep

Lt. Comdr. William A. Goss, U.S. Navy (Ret.) • 41 •
Keynote Speaker

Three years ago, Dr. Bob Fisher told a thirty-eight-year-old Navy pilot that he might never smile again. The little bump plucked from the pilot's ear was not a fatty cyst, as had been initially diagnosed, but was instead a deep melanoma—a deadly skin cancer caused by the sun.

Doctor Bob explained to the pilot that it was highly malignant and that removing it would require hours of drastic surgery on the face, neck, shoulder, and ear. Permanent facial paralysis was a real possibility (however long permanent might be for a person with such a bleak prognosis).

That Navy pilot was me.

When I first met with Dr. Fisher, it was like talking soul to soul. We had a connection: we were both Naval officers of the same age, we each had pretty wives, stable marriages, and two beautiful kids—a boy and a girl. We were two men with wonderful lives. The only difference was that one of us had cancer and the other could save him.

During our first meeting, he explained that I had two options. One operation would not guarantee that all the cancer would be removed. The other operation was massive and could mean that my face would be left paralyzed, and that I might lose the ability to smile.

When I asked Doctor Bob what had happened to other patients who had discovered melanomas on their ears, he looked away thoughtfully for a moment and said, "Well . . . one moved away . . . and . . . the other, well, I don't hear from him anymore."

As you can imagine, at that particular moment, his explanation was more than adequate. I didn't press him for details. I just took out photographs of my wife and kids and said, "Hey, I don't want to die. You have to help me 'cause you know where I'm coming from." I could tell how much this touched him. Then I asked, "What would you do if you were in my shoes?"

He said, "I don't know what to say, but if you were my son, I would tell you to do anything it takes to live." That left a strong impression on me. I was thinking, *Why is he looking at me as his son when we are the same age?* Then I realized that, because our lives were so similar, it would have been too much for him to imagine himself in my shoes. It was easier for him to see me as his son.

I knew he was days away from retirement and asked if someone else would be performing the operation. He said, "No, Bill, I will be your surgeon. I'll be leaving the Navy a couple of days later, but I will be with you until then." He could have given the surgery to another doctor, but he didn't. He knew he was the person to save me.

I was putting my life in the hands of a doctor who wore beat-up docksiders that were so worn his toes stuck out of them. He was like a character from *M.A.S.H.* He didn't adhere to Navy regulations and wasn't into protocol: he was just into being in that operating room and doing his job well.

The Navy wanted me to fly to Bethesda, Maryland's giant Naval hospital, for my operation. Bethesda had a reputation for having the finest specialists in this type of surgery. But I knew that Dr. Bob would do whatever it took to make sure I would be around to watch my kids grow up. We had a special connection and I believed in him.

Because he was leaving the Navy in just a few days and moving his family across the country, he had every reason to have his mind elsewhere—but he didn't. He could have done my operation in five or six hours, which was typical for this kind of surgery, but he spent twelve. Had he rushed, he could have missed a lymph node or knicked a nerve. He removed over two hundred lymph nodes, two salivary glands, a trapezius muscle, a jugular vein, and half an ear. All the while, he carefully—and I mean *very* carefully—tried to avoid nicking any of the tiny nerves that are embedded like spiderwebs throughout the face and neck—nerves that if cut, would leave my face paralyzed and prevent me from being able to smile again.

Even though the Navy hadn't recommended that he do this extensive operation, he had been determined to do it. The nurses took breaks during the long and tedious surgery, but Dr.

Bob did not. You see, I was his baby, his responsibility, and his goal was to deliver me, twelve hours later, cancer-free and un-paralyzed, to the recovery room.

When I woke up after the operation, Dr. Bob was standing over me. The first thing he said was, "Bill, make an 'O' with your lips and then blow." I did it, and then I saw a big smile on his face. He said quietly, "Thank God." It meant that he was confident I would eventually get back my smile. It also meant that he had done his job well. To me, being a surgeon is like being a mechanic. Being a fine surgeon is like being an artist. Dr. Bob was a true artist.

The following morning a nurse came into my room and, while tucking in my sheets, said, "Your surgery was unbeliev-able. We could all tell Dr. Fisher cared so much about you. He always does everything so fast, but when he was in that operat-ing room, he slowed down and took such care with you. He was determined to save your life."

I'll never forget when Dr. Bob walked in with the good news. He had sent a bag of frozen lymph nodes to Bethesda, and there was no trace of cancer. This meant that my chances of living were very good. He shook my hand, looked me in the eye, and said, "My job is done." The next day, he was gone.

It took four or five months for my smile to completely re-turn. I would have been glad simply to be alive, but the smile represented the preservation of my soul and my personality. Dr. Bob knew that.

I found out that he had moved to Minnesota, but when I

tried to reach him, I learned that he had moved further north, deep into Alaska.

Wherever you are now, Dr. Bob (could be the North Pole for all I know), I want to say thank you for being my Earth Angel— and I'm saying this with the biggest, broadest smile you've ever seen! I believe that all doctors and nurses, at some time in their careers, serve as Earth Angels. Dr. Bob Fisher was an extraordinarily gifted doctor who went above and beyond for me.

I'd like to leave you with this little poem (with apologies to Robert Frost)—

> *The woods are lonely dark and deep,*
> *but I have promises to keep,*
> *And smiles to go before I sleep,*
> *And smiles to go before I sleep.*

How Are You?

Rachel • 33 • Magazine Editor

For over a year, I was not fine.

When my boyfriend unexpectedly left me, my family and friends tried to make me feel better. They said things like,

"He was no good," "You wouldn't want someone who would leave you," "Don't worry, you'll find someone much better."

Nothing they said or did made me feel better. My life felt so empty.

I was confused, especially because, even after he left, he would tell me how much he loved me. Late at night, we would sometimes cry on the phone together.

He had recently started seeing a psychologist to deal with bad memories of his childhood (his father was an alcoholic). He was struggling to understand his life, and I guess our relationship became extra baggage on an important journey that he had to make alone.

Six months after he left, he was still very much alive in my heart. I didn't feel any better and I couldn't seem to move on with my own life. I knew he wasn't coming back, but our love was trapped in a bad place inside of me.

After a year my friends and family began to lose patience with me. They wanted to make me feel angry at him or distract me by introducing me to other men.

Then one day, something unexpected happened. An older gentleman, who works at the other end of the hall from me, paused at my cubicle and asked, "How are you?"

We had previously smiled in passing, but never stopped.

People are always asking each other, "How are you?" But it's usually just a way of saying, "Hi." Most people don't really want the answer and, even if they do, people do not always respond honestly. They simply say, "Fine," even if they are not. But on this particular day, in response to a gentleman whose name I didn't know, I answered honestly.

"Not so good," I said. "The man I love left me more than a year ago. I know I should move on and live my life, but I can't seem to, no matter how hard I try. When you truly love someone, it's not easy to get them out of your system even if they are physically gone." I gulped. I couldn't believe all this came out of me to a virtual stranger. All he had asked was, "How are you?" Should I have just said, "Fine"? Well, it was too late now.

I looked into his eyes for a sign. I was relieved to see that he didn't seem at all uncomfortable with my openness.

He gave me a warm smile and nodded. Then he stepped closer and said, "It must have really hurt when he left you. This past year must have been very difficult for you."

These words sank into me. No one had ever acknowledged my pain. Those around me just wanted me to move on, get over it, find someone else. They didn't allow me to *feel*.

He continued to speak and his gentle words taught me a lesson I carry with me: "I don't believe you should try to get him out of your system. That will never work. You will always feel that you have failed. The people we love stay with us, even if they are gone. Allow a place in your heart for that love to rest."

I was so speechless that I could barely say, "Thank you."

He smiled his warm smile and continued down the hall.

He never stopped by again, and I rarely saw him in passing. But the few times I did see him, we gave each other a warm smile.

It's amazing what can happen when you open up to someone and truthfully answer the question, "How are you?" It can make a significant difference in your life, as it did in mine. That someone could be an Earth Angel with important and healing words.

I pull out his advice when I talk with people who have lost a loved one, and it never fails to make them feel better. To know that you can let someone go without creating a gaping hole makes it possible to live in a world where loss is inevitable.

I now know why my boyfriend left and never came back: it was so I would be free and willing to open up, when the time was right, to meet my soul mate. I did, and we have been happily married for more than two years.

Stay

Stephanie A. Felling • 54 • Artist

"What is to give light must first endure burning."
—*Victor Frankl*

I was a volunteer at a Veterans Administration hospital. Every Wednesday afternoon I spent a few hours going from ward to ward talking with Vietnam veterans. Some of them had very few visitors.

I don't remember what prompted me to get involved as a volunteer. Quiet, reserved, and painfully shy, I normally avoided any unpleasantness, conflict, or confrontation. I was not formally trained as a psychologist, nor was I experienced in dealing professionally with this sort of situation. Perhaps I had read an item in the newspaper or seen something on TV that lit a spark in me. I felt somehow mysteriously compelled to follow through with this idea even though I knew it would be difficult.

The first time I saw him, he was still groggy from surgery. Before I entered his room, the nurse informed me of his condition. "He's got Hodgkin's disease," she said. She shook her head sadly. "It doesn't look good. It's very advanced. He's only twenty-three years old. It goes fast in the young ones. His name is Tommy."

In Vietnam he had been a warrior in places no gentle soul would want to go. He had been seriously wounded twice, but after each recovery, he was ordered back to combat. He was trained to be an effective, efficient killer. Many of his buddies never made it home. He was haunted by them and by what he had done in Vietnam.

The second time I saw Tommy, he was awake. Even though he had been groggy when we met, he remembered me from before. "Do you know what I have?" he asked bluntly.

"Yes," I replied, hesitantly.

"Do you feel sorry for me?" There was no avoiding the intensity in his eyes.

"No," I replied, "but I do admire your courage." I noticed the tension in his shoulders relax.

"Good," he said. "I don't want anybody's pity." His doctor had left only moments before, after telling Tommy his prognosis. He knew how bad it was. He told me that his mother was due to visit in a few minutes, and he asked me to stay.

When she arrived, she greeted him casually. She seemed remote, distant. I felt awkward, like an intruder. "Mom, I need to talk to you," he said. "It's really important." He reminded me of a little boy who had to tell his mother that he had just broken the neighbor's window or gotten into trouble at school.

She avoided his eyes and searched the room nervously for something else to focus on.

I made the motions of getting ready to leave, and he insisted again that I stay.

"When your brother Jack gets here," she said, "tell him I

forgot to unplug the coffee pot. I've got to go," she said as she edged closer to the door. "I'm late for work. I have to hurry. I can't stay. I'll be back to see you later." He did not protest.

As soon as she left, he breathed a sigh of relief. I felt like crying. She hadn't given him the chance to tell her how ill he really was. I suspect she already knew in her heart and it was too difficult for her to face.

"Last night I had a dream about my grandmother," he told me. "She's been dead for a long time. In my dream she spoke to me." I knew that he had spent the first nine years of his life with her in Harlin County, Kentucky—way back in the hills.

I was curious. "What did she say?" I asked.

"Be humblin', boy."

I didn't understand. "What does that mean?" I asked.

"It means to be humble, be kind and loving, be a good person," he said. His voice softened as he described his grandmother and how much he had loved her.

He told me that he had a chemotherapy treatment scheduled that afternoon.

"You don't have to leave yet, do you? It would mean a lot to me if you could stay."

What was this power he was beginning to have over me? I was reluctant to abandon him, but at the same time I was afraid to stay.

"They use a derivative of cobra snake venom and mustard gas," he said matter-of-factly. "They just add it to my IV."

The thought horrified me. He had already been through this once before, so he knew what to expect. Then someone in a white uniform came into the room and, in a very impersonal, businesslike manner, added the potent poisons to the flow of liquid dripping into the vein in his right arm and walked away.

"Come sit here by my bed and talk to me," he said softly. "Stay if you can, until the chemo starts having an effect." As he spoke, the veins in his arm began to bulge. Soon his whole upper body was flushed and his chest was heaving with the wild, rapid thumping of his heart. I was afraid for him. I wanted to calm him, to comfort him, to soothe the violent physical reactions that were increasing rapidly and dramatically. I was alone with him. Where were the doctors, or nurses—someone, anyone, to help him?

He had been lying there with his eyes closed. He stirred and said, "You'd better leave now. This stuff makes me really sick, and I don't want you to see me throwing up."

Then I touched his arm. At that instant—in a flash—my life was changed forever. In my heart I knew with absolute certainty that I didn't care what it took, or what it cost, I wanted to be with this man until the day he died. Within me, there was a sensation of completion, as if a major missing piece of a jigsaw puzzle had suddenly fallen into place. It felt like he was the other half of my self.

We were married and lived together for exactly one year and three days. Because of Tommy, I became a person of tremendous inner strength and courage. These were his gifts to me.

I was with him when he died in our home, as I had promised him. It was Thanksgiving Day.

Tommy was my Earth Angel and I have felt his presence as my guardian angel ever since.

Ann and Andy

Linda Ward Barrett • 35 • Keynote Speaker and Seminar Leader

My parents and I had just walked into the Trinity College Chapel in Washington, D.C., for the opening ceremonies that would mark the beginning of my freshman year. Other eager students and their families filed into the church around us. I was deep in thought about what the next four years would bring.

Suddenly I was shaken back into reality when I saw her.

She was engaged in an animated conversation with the people around her. She was the only one in her group who looked my age. Unlike me, however, she would be experiencing the next four years from a wheelchair.

I decided I wanted to meet her, so after the ceremony, I introduced myself. Her name was Ann Kurz, and she had cerebral palsy, an affliction that affects motor development. Although her body was unable to do many things most people tend to take for granted, her mind and spirit were strong and vibrant. She casually mentioned that she was the first wheelchair-bound woman to attend the college. I immediately felt an affinity for this woman who was boldly blazing new trails for other wheelchair-bound individuals.

When the opportunity to become one of her aids presented itself, I jumped at the chance. For the next few years I helped Ann with her daily activities, while she taught me lessons about life.

Her wit and charm made her delightful to be around. Her favorite song was "To Dream the Impossible Dream." One of the many lessons Ann taught me was that "handicapped" is a relative term. She helped me understand that, in one way or another, we all fit the description.

Ann graduated from Trinity College with honors, and successfully landed a job. In her annual Christmas letter she reminds me that any one of us can dare to dream the impossible dream.

It was seven years ago when I realized that Ann was my Earth Angel.

In the seventh month of my otherwise normal pregnancy, my water suddenly broke. Five days later I gave birth to a three-pound baby boy whose lungs were not fully developed. Our fragile little Andy was in severe respiratory distress. The doctors predicted that he would not live through the night.

Something made me think of Ann. As I drifted to sleep that

night, I dared to dream the impossible dream. The next morning I awoke to the wonderful news. Andy had lived.

Over the next several days he continued to grow stronger, but a couple of weeks later, a doctor told us Andy had suffered a major brain hemorrhage. Then, several months after that, he was diagnosed with cerebral palsy.

Because of my Earth Angel named Ann, I am better able to understand and see the miracle of my little boy named Andy.

Ann and Andy met for the first time at our college reunion; it was very touching. Andy's greatest asset is that he is very sociable. He loves being around people, and the moment he saw Ann, he wanted to give her a big hug. The two of them smiled at each other and, through my tears, I could see their instant connection.

Andy is starting to walk now and we're working on his communication skills. Knowing all that Ann has accomplished in her life gives me hope for Andy's future.

The Girl Who Made Us a Family

Joan Urban • 46 • Mother, formerly Marketing Director

The first time we saw Rene, she was sitting in a fast-food restaurant in Phoenix, bathed in a mixture of sunlight and fluorescent glare. Her chair was pulled as close to the table as her watermelon-big belly would allow, and parked close to her in a stroller was a toddler, slumped in sleep.

Phil and I had just traveled two thousand miles to meet the voice we'd talked to six or seven times by phone over the past month. Rene had called our New York City apartment late one February night to say she'd seen our ad in the Phoenix newspaper: *Couple Hoping to Adopt . . .*

Her voice was surprisingly calm and steady, I thought—flat almost—as she succinctly related the facts of her situation. She was almost eighteen years old, six months pregnant with twins, and unable to continue working due to pregnancy complications; she lived in a small trailer with her fifteen-month-old daughter.

I was breathless with hope and nervousness as she spoke, and I could barely hear her voice through the thumping sound of the heartbeat in my ears. But Rene remained coolly controlled, wasting little conversation in chitchat. I had prepared a whole case history of my infertility trials to pour out to anyone who responded to our ad—the DES exposure that probably led to massive uterine fibroids, the many surgeries that removed the fibroids but left scar tissue, the volleys of hormone shots, the failed in vitros, the frozen embryos that died thawing in their petri dishes, on and on "ad miseriam"—but in that first phone call we stuck pretty much to the matters at hand.

By her second call Rene had already talked to our adoption attorney, as I had suggested; by the third call she had asked her doctor to send us copies of her medical records. On the fourth phone call, she asked to meet us. We were ecstatic at the implied commitment of such a meeting, and at the chance to see what this stalwart agent of our dreams looked like. Phil and I booked flights for the following weekend. In her last call to us before the trip, Rene designated our point of rendezvous—the Burger King on Alameda Avenue, twelve noon.

And there she was. She sat at the table closest to the glass entry doors, her arms stretched out stiffly on the Formica tabletop, her fingers tightly woven. Her mouth was a long, thin line of determination, but her eyes, when she looked at us coming through the doors, were worlds of fear and confusion. I could see everything that her flat voice had been hiding.

That weekend, in the melting heat of Arizona, we gradually became more at ease with each other. The strain of wanting to be perfectly honest, while saying the right thing, had my brain in a painful buzz, but the three of us did manage to share some history of ourselves, see some striking desert scenery, and even have a few laughs over tacos. When Rene placed my hand on the globe of her belly to feel the riot of kicking within, I knew she had chosen us as the parents-in-waiting.

Two months later, Phil and I hovered at Rene's bedside in the Phoenix Community Birthing Center. The friend she had picked as a labor partner hadn't shown up, so we were recruited! Phil coached Rene's breathing in an untrained but enthusiastic manner—more a cheerleader than a coach, really—while I pushed mightily on her back to lessen the pain. I did my best to drown her screams with soothing words and to smooth back the long blond hair in tangles around her head.

Ten hours later Rene lay back quietly on the peach-colored sheets of the postdelivery beds. Phil and I sat anxiously perched in chairs on either side of her. We tensed as two nurses entered the room, each with a freshly swaddled infant. They lowered the babies toward Rene's arms, but she shook her head. "No," she said, smiling at the twin packages, "they should be with their parents now."

Our children are four years old now, and soon they'll want to know more about their beginnings and the person who carried them into life. We made scrapbooks for them about their birth and adoption, and saved all photographs and letters from Rene. They will easily find their likeness to her: the straight blond hair, the broad cheekbones, the wide, curling smile. The gifts are easy to see. But what our Earth Angel gave to us as parents—the millions of brightly-colored moments that will arrange themselves into a lifetime—these things we could never begin to count.

A Box in the Attic

Jacklin • *36* • *Photographer*

My friend was leaving work one Friday evening, looking forward to spending the long holiday weekend with her fiancé.

As she was getting into her car in the empty and enclosed parking structure, a tall young man approached her from behind. He put a knife to her throat and demanded, "Get in the passenger's seat and give me the keys!" She had no choice but to obey.

The next two days were filled with torture too gruesome to mention. She was sure she would die. He kept insisting he was going to kill her.

Finally, on Sunday, he threw her into the car and began driving on a remote highway. My friend was sobbing uncontrollably when the man decided to push her out of the moving car. She felt her body tumble along the ground without any energy to resist the impact.

She was bloody and her clothes were torn almost completely from her body. She managed to pick herself up and walk, without any idea where to go. She just knew that if she didn't keep going, she might die.

Finally, in the distance, she saw a building. As she approached it, she could see a guard running toward her.

As he got closer, she started to scream, because he looked like the man who had kidnapped her. Her legs wouldn't hold her up any longer, and as she began to collapse, the man said to her, "It's okay, I want to help you!" He caught her in his arms and gently laid her on the ground. He took off his jacket and wrapped her in it. Then she saw him run to a pay phone in front of the building, where he called for an ambulance.

Several months passed, and my friend's wounds were healing—including, slowly, the emotional scars. She remembered looking up at the guard's kind face before the ambulance took her away. She wanted to thank him, not only for coming to her rescue, but for helping her realize that there are good people and there are bad people, regardless of what they look like. Without him, she was afraid she may have grown to hate and be fearful of anyone resembling her attacker.

The woman and her fiancé decided to drive out to the building where the guard worked, so they could return the jacket. She had pinned a little golden angel to the lapel as a small token of her appreciation.

They found the building but, before my friend got out of the car, she paused. This horrible memory was a lot for her to face, but her desire to thank the man gave her the strength to continue.

They didn't see the guard outside, so they went into the building. There was a receptionist at the front desk who looked up as soon as the door closed behind them.

"Can I help you?" she asked.

"Yes, we're looking for the guard who works here," my friend's fiancé responded.

"Guard? We have no guard."

"Yes, but . . ."

"I'm sorry, you must have the wrong building," the receptionist continued. "I've been working here for twelve years and we've never had a guard."

"I'm sure this is the building," my friend spoke up. "There isn't another building like this for miles." She held up the jacket. "This belongs to him. He let me borrow it."

"Well, is there a name on it?" asked the receptionist.

"No." My friend looked down and clutched the jacket in her arms.

"Come on, honey." Her fiancé's voice was soothing. He put his arm around her shoulder. "Let's go home."

On the drive back, they were quiet. As they walked into the house, my friend said, "The whole way home I just kept thinking, and I know it sounds strange, but . . . ," she paused, "maybe he was an angel."

She took the guard's jacket and put it in a box in the attic.

It has been several years since that terrible incident. The couple is now happily married, and they have a beautiful little girl.

When my friend heard about this book, she wanted me to tell the story for her. She wanted to thank the guard, wherever he is, and tell him that she will always remember his kindness and the lesson she learned from her tragic experience.

My Angel in Blue

George Guizar • 17 • Goal: Law Enforcement Officer

One summer, a couple of friends and I were playing soccer at a park near my house. The ball was accidentally kicked into the street and I went after it. As I ran into the street, I was hit by a truck and knocked unconscious.

Moments later, when full vision returned, I remember looking around for a face that could bring comfort. When I looked up, there was a tall, uniformed man standing above me. Even though he had a big build, he was like a large, soft teddy bear.

As he kneeled down beside me, he said, "Everything is going to be all right." Then he touched my hand and a bolt of electricity ran through my body; for a while, the pain seemed to go away. When the paramedics arrived, the uniformed man let go of my hand, and all of a sudden the pain returned.

The first person waiting for me in the emergency room was this same man, Officer Gonzales. As I was taken to the operating room to have two broken ribs repaired, he held my hand until the doctors instructed him to let go, but I noticed that he was hesitant.

I came out of the operating room three hours later, and I looked for that angelic face, but it wasn't there. I remember thinking even then, that he must have been an angel.

About half an hour before visiting hours were over, I saw

Officer Gonzales standing in the doorway, but this time he wasn't alone. By his side was the most beautiful woman in the world, Mrs. Ana Gonzales, and in her hands was a cake. In the officer's hands was a brand new soccer ball.

It was then that I realized that angels aren't only people who can fly and perform miracles. Angels can be real people who are there to give a warm smile and a healing hand.

She Led Me Home

Martin • 34 • Graphic Artist

I was invited to a get-together on Christmas Eve. It was a tradition a small group of friends had started several years earlier.

I was going through something that I didn't feel like sharing. Although these people were my good friends, I was extremely depressed and knew I would have to pretend I was happy so they wouldn't suspect that anything was wrong.

Reluctantly I went. When I arrived, we said our hellos and I was introduced to a couple of people I had never met. Throughout dinner one of the women kept my attention. I noticed how open she was, and, when she caught me staring, she gave me a warm smile.

After dinner we all sat down in the living room. Part of our tradition was talking about what we all wanted for the coming year. I knew what I wanted and I also knew I couldn't tell anyone.

A couple of people decided to go outside and look at the stars. I told them I would be out in a minute as did the woman, Lillian. We were both sitting on the couch; she was reading a book she had picked up from the table, and I was deep in thought. She put down the book and looked at me.

"So how long have you been living in San Francisco?" she asked.

"About seven years," I answered.

"I don't mean to be personal, but when everyone was saying what they wanted for the coming year, you were vague. What do you do for a living?"

Ordinarily I would have felt she was prying. But watching her during the evening, the way she listened and cared about what everyone was saying, made me feel comfortable.

"I am a graphic artist. I really like what I do. It's just that I don't like who I'm working for."

"Well," her voice was optimistic, "just work harder a little longer and in a few years you can start your own business."

"I won't be able to do that," I told her. I could feel tears forming in my eyes. I couldn't believe I felt so comfortable.

"Why not?" she asked quietly, as if she already knew.

I could barely get the words out: "I have the illness."

I couldn't even say the word.

"Oh," she said. "How advanced is it?"

"I may only have a few months. They don't really know. I haven't told anyone. The only person who knows is the nurse who's been trying to help me cope. She's been great."

"What about your family? Haven't you told them?"

"No. My parents don't even know I'm gay. I'm from a small town in Virginia and they wouldn't understand. That's why I came here." I couldn't believe I was telling this stranger things I hadn't even told my friends.

"I think you should go home, Marty." She looked directly into my eyes. "I know I'm not sitting where you are, but imagine how your parents would feel not being able to say good-bye. It would be easier for them if they were able to take care of you. I don't know them, but you seem like a good person. Part of that had to come from your parents."

"My parents *are* good people. That's why I wouldn't want to hurt them."

"Then go home," she interrupted. "Go home and give them a chance to love you before you leave this world."

I just sat there trying to hold back the tears.

Then she took my hand. I hadn't wanted to touch anyone because, even though one can't contract AIDS by touching, I felt uncomfortable. She was so brave, and she must have known how much I needed human contact. I remember sitting there for a long time, holding this woman's hand and letting her words sink in.

The evening was over and we were all saying good-bye. Lillian came over to me and hugged me. I pulled back for a second, then I let myself sink into her caring embrace. She whispered in my ear, "Good luck, Marty. I'll keep you in my prayers."

"Thank you," I said. "I appreciate everything you said tonight. I will try to take your advice."

We let go and she gave me another warm smile.

The next week, the day after the New Year, I found myself giving my roommate notice, calling all my friends, and telling them about my condition and that I was going home to Virginia. My parents were the only ones who didn't know I was coming—or why. I sold my car and took a plane.

I'll never forget the walk up my driveway. It had been such a long time since I had been home. The trees looked bigger and the house seemed so inviting. All the curtains were open, and the sun was shining through the trees, casting beautiful shadows on the Victorian porch.

It wasn't easy to tell my parents, but Lillian was right. They did not judge me, they simply held me and cried with me.

It has been a year and a half since I went home. I am doing okay. The new drugs seem to help. My parents have been doing whatever they can for me, and I have started a small graphic design business.

I don't know how long I have on this earth, but I want to thank Lillian, wherever she is. I want to tell her that I admire her honesty and I appreciate her caring advice more than she knows. I will never forget my Earth Angel, Lillian. If I ever see her again, I won't hesitate to hug her.

Chapter 6

Heroes Among Us

A boy doesn't have to go to war to be a hero;
He can say he doesn't like pie when he sees
there isn't enough to go around.

—Ed Howe

When we first began writing Earth Angels, we were finding the stories one at a time. But, within a few months, our book had begun to fly. Earth Angels was reaching people everywhere! We never got over being surprised and delighted when we discovered a mound of mail stuffed into our post office box, or came home to find several messages on our Earth Angels Hotline. In much of the correspondence we received, people asked for our Web address.

Web address? Why not! Being on the Worldwide Web would

mean that Earth Angels could be instantaneously invited into the homes of numerous people in cities and towns all around the globe.

It didn't take us long to decide how we wanted our web page to look: the planet earth as seen from outer space with people of all races encircling it and holding hands.

It was close to midnight one night, when we ventured onto the Internet to try to find our page. We went to SEARCH and typed in: EARTH ANGELS.

What appeared on the screen was a listing for Earth Angels, but it wasn't ours. We sent a midnight message, by e-mail, to the organization's director, inviting him to contribute to our book.

The next morning, we received an e-mail message from him that read: "I was thrilled to receive your invitation. Your book is long overdue! Our Earth Angels would be proud to join yours. We need more people committed to celebrating the positive side of life. Though there are many Earth Angels who stand out in my mind, somehow Anthony has always seemed particularly special. He is not only an Earth Angel, he is one of the Earth's silent heroes."

In our society we have a need for heroes. They exemplify the true meaning of strength and courage, and demonstrate how we can reach beyond the ordinary boundaries of human kindness. Heroes can inspire us to realize our own potential and to take action beyond the call of duty.

Though we believe every Earth Angel is in some way a hero, and every person has the potential to be one, this chapter is dedicated to heroes like Anthony, who instinctively give of themselves and sometimes risk their lives under extraordinary circumstances.

An Angel Among Angels

Neil S. Andre • 47 • Director, Environmental Association

Nine years ago I founded a pre-teen inner city group of "at risk" children helping an "at risk" world. Our group is called The Earth Angels of Guardian Angel Settlement Association. We have become nationally known as a result of our constant efforts to help the rapidly graying earth. Today there are four Earth Angel groups operating out of the worst inner city areas of St. Louis. These areas have the highest preponderance of gangs, drugs, and drive-by shootings. Just to live in these areas, is to live in constant jeopardy.

These kids are able to look beyond the graffiti-stained walls and asphalt streets and see a planet in need of their care. It is from the ranks of The Earth Angels that I have chosen my *special* Earth Angel—a difficult task with so many to choose from.

Anthony was ten years old and hanging around the fringes of a gang when he asked to join our group. At first some of the staff felt he had been too damaged to help in a group where members give much of themselves, while receiving little in return.

He had already had more than his share of adversity. He lived in a decaying house that was packed with twenty members of his extended family, and the house was constantly filled with screaming and shouting. He often mentioned that he wished he could have a closet at home so that he could study or just sit and have some peace.

Somehow Anthony's penetrating eyes convinced me that he had more to give than anyone believed.

Once he became a member, Anthony quickly began to work on projects as if he was driven: he would not even stop to drink a soda or rest. Once, the day before summer school started, he was digging rocks out of a habitat we were developing. The other volunteers were playing kickball after having done a major work project that morning. I casually suggested that he might enjoy joining the game, and he said, "This is my last day for a few weeks. I want to get more work done for the earth."

As soon as summer school ended, Anthony was back with us and working as hard as ever.

Around that time, a wealthy contributor offered to have T-shirts made with our logo for all the group members; he also said he would be willing to make a large donation. Then the other shoe dropped. In return he wanted us to stop our "silly boycott of fur."

Though I dreaded it, I knew that it was only fair to have the kids make the decision. They went from being ecstatic to dumbfounded in one of the longest discussions they had ever had. I tried to make it easier for them by saying that I doubted our boycott was doing much good anyway. Finally Anthony spoke, and his strong words convinced the others to stay with their convictions.

Several days later Anthony came in with a beautifully written article about why we should boycott fur and asked if we could include it in our next newsletter. I not only included it, I made sure it was on the front page!

A few weeks later Anthony's older brother, who had taken such good care of him, was accidentally killed in a drive-by shooting. Before Anthony could let this loss sink in, one of his cousins, who had been living with him, was killed while playing basketball. Again, a case of mistaken identity.

The three teens who killed Anthony's brother were caught and identified by several witnesses. In court, however, their gang showed up and sat near the front of the courtroom. Witness after witness was suddenly unable to identify them (the police said, if they had, they would have been dead for sure), so they were released. Anthony confided to me how difficult it was to see his brother's killers in the neighborhood every day.

Throughout the next few months, Anthony adjusted to his loss. Instead of withdrawing into depression, which would have made sense, he became amazingly active. He persuaded the group to send money to Sarah Brady's Gun Control Incorporated to get semi-automatic rapid-fire guns off the street. Then he did a very courageous and admirable thing—he wrote about the loss of his brother and cousin, and appealed to the public. Instead of retaliating, he wanted people to find other ways of dealing with the violence in their lives.

One evening I heard a commotion coming from the street. I raced outside to see Anthony trying to keep five older teens from getting to a pigeon that couldn't fly. When they saw me, they reluctantly walked away. Anthony pleaded with me to help him save the bird. When I said, "You must love pigeons," he shrugged and told me that it was a living thing and we should care for all living things.

Anthony is now nineteen and divides his time among several organizations. He has taken the devastating and negative things that have happened to him and turned them around. Anthony continues to make a positive difference for the earth and all of us living here. Whenever I need his help with The Earth Angels, I know that he will move mountains to be here.

The one person who would never see Anthony as an Earth Angel is Anthony himself. To me, that makes him a real angel among angels.

He Was Only Four

Melissa Mann • 14 • Goal: Photography

When I was very young, my mother tried to teach me how to swim. I loved it. Swimming may not seem like a very important thing to learn sometimes, but at other times it can be as important as someone's life.

Whenever I went swimming, I wore a red flotation bathing suit, and I wouldn't swim without it because I was too scared of the water.

One day, when I was about two, my mom was talking on the phone and watering the plants outside, while I was sitting inside watching a cartoon with my four-year-old brother. My mom had left open the sliding glass door leading into the lanai and pool. I decided to take a walk out onto the lanai to watch my mother.

Since I was a little girl and loved the attention I got whenever I tried to impress adults, I thought it would be fun to jump in the pool and show my mom how well I could swim without my red flotation bathing suit. So, leaving my brother to watch cartoons alone, I made my way to the pool.

I got right to the edge and flung my body into the water. For a few seconds I managed to stay afloat. But those few seconds were not long enough, and I started splashing around trying to breathe. Then I started to scream, cry, and panic. I splashed and twisted my little body, trying to get out of the water.

As soon as my mother heard the splash, she turned around to see me bobbing furiously in the water. She immediately dropped the phone and hose to make her way to the pool. But, on her first step, she fell face forward onto the lanai. (She had dropped the hose directly in front of her feet and tripped right over it.)

My brother did not remain mesmerized by the cartoons after he heard all the screaming. He ran outside to see what was causing the commotion and saw his poor little sister drowning in the pool.

So he did the first thing that came to mind—he jumped in and saved me from drowning! He swam to me as if he had been doing it all his life. He grabbed onto me and pulled me right out of the pool.

When my mother gained the strength to pull herself up, she noticed my brother holding me in his arms as I cried hysterically. She ran over to me, picked me up in her arms, and began rocking me back and forth.

At first she didn't even acknowledge that my brother had

saved me, until I started crying harder and reaching for him. She looked to see what I wanted so badly, and seeing that my brother was drenched, realized he had saved my life. She ran up to him with me in her arms and began to hug both of us as if she hadn't seen us in years.

My wonderful brother saved my life and I will never forget it. My brother, now sixteen years old, is my Earth Angel and the best brother I could possibly have.

In an Instant

Racheal • 17 • Goal: Movie Producer

Earth Angels, in all their glory, can be hard to believe in these days, but in a time when the world is full of hate and heinous crimes, untrustworthy kids and feeble adults, we humans are still able to produce good-hearted, loving people who make life worth living.

My mom and dad's relentless pursuit of being great parents made me believe in good-hearted people; my oldest brother showed me how to chase my dreams and my youngest brother taught me the meaning of tough love. But my Earth Angel is my brother, Dion.

One day Dion, my pregnant sister-in-law, and I were on our

way to the lake to go fishing. But first we stopped at a friend's house in a bad part of Los Angeles and when the visit was over, and we were heading to the car, someone pulled a drive-by on us!

I was already in the car, protected by the steel, but my brother and sister-in-law were not. As the shots rang out I looked up, hoping to see them safe. But what I saw was my brother heroically jumping in front of his wife—saving her and her unborn child—as he took six bullets and collapsed to the ground.

My brother saved two lives that day. My niece is now two, and her mother is happily remarried. Their lives go on, thanks to Dion. That's why he is an Earth Angel.

My brother, whom I love, had not always been perfect. God knows he had a trying life. I really didn't see him as an angel of any sort, until that awful morning in June. But as I watched him save his wife and unborn child, Dion grew wings and flew away, becoming an angel of both heaven and earth to me.

On Occom Pond

John Sterling • *44* • *Editor-in-Chief, Book Publisher*

I grew up in Hanover, New Hampshire, where Dartmouth College is, as a matter of fact—and I lived on a hill above a pond.

When I was young, I was a passionate hockey player. Every year I would wait with great anticipation for that day when the ice on Occom Pond was thick enough to skate on. It was difficult, sometimes, to hold out long enough for the ice to get four or five inches thick, but you knew if you didn't, you risked a soak in very cold water.

When it was finally possible to skate, I spent what seemed like every spare hour on this pond, which meant that I often skated under risky conditions. For instance, if the ice was slushy, I was out there; if it was absolutely freezing and even if it was snowing, I was out there.

One day, when I was about ten years old, I was playing hockey with some friends. We were having a pick-up game on a Saturday, and we had played for about forty-five minutes when it started snowing. It came down very suddenly—one of those beautiful, dry snows that you get when it's midwinter.

We kept playing until it was impossible to play any longer because the ice had become completely covered with snow. But I wasn't ready to quit. It was so beautiful that I kept skating. It was exhilarating to be out there on the ice, skating around the pond without my hockey stick in the cold New Hampshire winter.

My last memory, before the accident, was of a beautiful white curtain. The next thing I knew, I was on my back and groggily staring up at a circle of faces. A number of people were standing around me. My head hurt, and I was especially aware that my legs were in a bad way.

I picked up my head and saw that I had been run over by a snow blower! I realized that both of my legs were tangled in its spiral teeth.

The people who had gathered around me were obviously scared; I could see it in their faces. I was very scared too. There I was, looking at the mouth of a snow blower, in pain, and probably about to go into shock.

Everyone seemed helpless. They didn't know what to do, because they couldn't tell whether or not my legs were broken. They were, for the most part, a bunch of kids, as was the guy who had been pushing the snow blower. He was completely stunned.

All of us tried to assess the situation as best we could and discovered that, fortunately, one of my skates had hit the blade of the snow blower exactly perpendicularly. The skate blade had snapped and jammed the motor before it could rip up my legs. Thank God they had not been torn up, but were just badly tangled in the snow blower. I still had no idea if they were broken, nor did anyone else. I just knew that I had to get the skates off.

Then my Earth Angel stepped in.

There was a road around the pond, and walking along this road was a man who came down onto the ice. He was probably in his late sixties; he had iron-gray hair, crew-cut style; his face was thin and pale, but strong; and he had on wire-rim glasses. He was quiet, but commanding, and he gently but firmly took charge.

He bent down to me and pulled a dime out of his pocket. I'll never forget that dime. It was almost the color of his hair. He used that dime to unlace my skates and then he gently slipped my feet out of them. I don't remember exactly what he said. He just spoke quietly, and told me it was going to be all right. Within a few minutes he had extricated my feet from the skates and my legs from the machine.

When the police arrived and were helping me to their car, they asked a few questions about what had happened. The guy who ran over me began telling the story, and one or two of the people standing around helped with the details. When they came to the part about the man with the dime, everyone looked around, but he was nowhere to be seen. I have a vague memory of people craning their necks, looking this way and that, saying, "Where did that man go?" and, "Who was he?" No one knew the answer. He had simply disappeared.

I was whisked away to the emergency room where I got six

stitches, and the doctors discovered that, miraculously, my legs were not broken. They were badly bruised and I couldn't use them for a week, but people could hardly believe how unscathed I was.

During that week, everyone in town was talking about the man who had seemed to appear out of nowhere. It was astonishing that nobody knew him. This was a small community, a town of five thousand people, where everybody knew everybody. The police had seen him walking along the road when they drove to the scene of the accident, but they didn't know who he was. All the people at the pond had seen him, but they didn't know him either.

He didn't save my life, precisely, but he did, at an absolutely critical moment, appear from seemingly nowhere, take command of the situation, and reassure me that I would be okay. I still have no idea who he was, though I've always wondered.

As simple as the story is, all of us in the town considered it extraordinary.

Over the years I continue to think about him from time to time. Today, whenever I hold a dime, it brings out an emotional response. I am immediately reminded of my Earth Angel and the gifts of help and comfort he gave to a young boy.

From an Earth Angel, Comes an Earth Angel

Sharon Norem Miller • *55* • *Self-Employed Mother of Two*

It was the summer of my eleventh year, and I was in the front of the rambling old farmhouse talking with my father when the cars hit. I nearly jumped out of my skin when I heard the crash, which sounded like the sudden clap of thunder when lightning strikes. It had come from the two-lane interstate, over a mile away, and we knew from the sound that it had to be bad.

"Accident," my father yelled as he ran to his pickup. I ran alongside him.

"Stay here," he demanded.

"No," I yelled back as I jumped into the cab and stared straight ahead, afraid he would force me to stay behind. But at that moment, my father's only concern was getting there.

He drove fast down the dirt road, and we seemed to reach the highway in seconds. A large-model Cadillac, badly mangled, blocked both lanes of traffic. The front end was pushed back almost into the windshield and dashboard. My father quickly raced to the crumpled vehicle, while I stayed in the truck, watching in horror as he courageously tried to open one of the tangled and broken doors. Finally, I forced myself to get out of the truck to try to help him. The air stank from the smell of burning oil and rubber.

A couple, younger than my parents, was lodged in what was

left of the front seat. Their heads poked clumsily through the glass of the broken windshield. The driver's eyes were closed, the woman's wide open and staring blankly into space. An older man and woman were in the back. The impact from the front seat had pinned them in an awkward position. Their eyes, too, were open and vacant, and instinctively, I knew that the passengers of this car were all dead.

But I was wrong. In the back seat, beneath the grandmother's skirt, a six-month-old baby lay partially hidden. The grandmother's body had shielded the infant at the moment of impact. From the sound of the baby's cries, it seemed frightened, but okay. I watched my father struggle with the twisted metal, trying to get to the trapped child. The smell of blood was overwhelming.

I looked around and saw the second car lying upside-down in the ditch alongside the highway. The roof had buckled and I could smell gasoline. A few yards ahead of me, at the side of the road, lay its driver. The man was young, in his late teens or early twenties. He was on his back, his military uniform torn and bloody. His head was covered in blood and a few flies were circling, landing, and circling again.

I walked toward him and noticed that his chest was moving. He was alive. Both eyes were closed, maybe from the strong midday sun. I knelt beside him and, as my shadow fell across his face, he opened his eyes.

Startled, I held my breath, afraid to move away, afraid to stay. He searched my face, unable to speak. At that moment my father's image as he strained to rescue the child gave me the will to go on. My fear disappeared. Carefully I brushed the flies away, watching him watch me. I tried to smile, knowing my presence was somehow comforting to him.

The air was completely still and silent. The only sound came from the buzzing of the flies.

The boy's body was badly broken; even I, a child, could see that. I laid my hand on his chest to feel his breath. At that moment, touching him the way I did, I sensed that he was going to die.

"I'll stay with you," I whispered.

I gently picked up his head and cradled it in my arms. He tried to smile, grateful for this kindness. Behind me I heard more cars and pickup trucks arrive. Other farmers had heard the terrible crash and come to help. I heard sirens in the distance. Someone had called for help, I thought, grateful.

A neighbor came up behind me and offered to step in.

"No," I told him, refusing to leave the boy.

"Let me help."

"I'll take care of him," I said.

The farmer walked away without another word, and went to help my father, who was still struggling with the doors on the Cadillac. Once again the young soldier opened his eyes. I heard a strange sound and leaned forward, in case he was trying to speak to me. Then I heard a second sound and, at last, a great gurgling rush of wind escaped his lips. I watched in amazement as his life force ebbed away.

Surprisingly I didn't cry. I sat with him, not moving, until the ambulance arrived. Then I heard the sheriff tell my father to take me home. As we walked to the truck, I didn't look back, even once, at the twisted wrecks or at the dead man lying there.

Much later, I learned that the soldier had been sent home to his family in Kansas, where he was buried with military honors. I know this because his family wrote to us, thanking us for our small kindness to their son at the end of his life. The family in the other car was returned to Florida for burial. As for the baby, it remained in the local hospital under observation for a few days, and was finally released into the care of a close relative.

Not only had I witnessed a life saved, I had seen death face-to-face and, for some reason, I hadn't been afraid. The end of life wasn't ugly or frightening, but a turning point. I began to understand.

My father was an Earth Angel—not only to the accident victims, but to me. Without saying a word, he taught me much that day. He was a man of few words, but his heart, as well as his hands, spoke volumes—on that day and so many times before. When a hobo, hungry and tired, wandered to our farm, for an hour or so of simple labor, my father made sure he was fed and clothed.

And when a pair of road-weary missionaries on a religious journey found themselves (in the dead of winter, with temperatures dipping well below freezing) in a snowbound countryside more cruel than the farmers who had chased them to our home, my father insisted that they stay the night, as our guests, and I remember the stimulating conversation in the morning. My father made sure that there was always a cup of hot cocoa at our table for a stranger. These are good memories.

My father was no saint by earthly standards, but if God in all his wisdom ever said, "Well done," to anyone, surely it would have been to this gentle hero.

In His Footsteps

Connie Howard • *Director of Special Projects at
Indiana University of Pennsylvania*

Manibhai Desai is a man whose life was changed by his friendship with Mahatma Gandhi. In turn, Manibhai Desai's friendship with me changed my life and my attitudes about what is truly important.

On one of my trips to India, Dr. P. R. Karmarkar ("Jake"), a professor at the University of Poona, who had worked with me on my India projects (including BAIF), said he'd like me to meet BAIF's founder, Manibhai Desai. It was arranged, and Jake and I went to BAIF headquarters in Pune.

When we arrived, Manibhai told us he couldn't visit with us for long since he had another meeting. He invited us to sit with him in the boardroom, and I immediately began talking and asking questions. Manibhai was quiet and seemed a little with-drawn, and I thought, *Oh, dear, he doesn't like me.*

I said, "You have no idea how much I admire you for the work you are doing and the fact that thousands of rural poor will live better lives because of you." I think he saw the sincer-ity in my face and heard it in my voice, because he suddenly smiled at me, and it was as though a wall between us had fallen away.

He began to talk freely, answering my questions, and telling me stories.

I looked at my watch several times and said, "Oh, dear, you'd better leave or you'll be late for your next meeting."

He just smiled, waved his hand in dismissal, and told me not to worry about it.

Jake finally stood and announced that we'd best be going. Manibhai and I also rose, but we kept talking as we walked out of the room, down the steps, and out onto the sidewalk. At one point I took his hand and said, "I'd really like to interview you on video and help spread the word in any way I can about the fantastic work you are doing. Maybe even write a book with you about your work some day."

He smiled and said, "All right."

We met briefly several other times, in Pune and when we were all in New Delhi. Fascinating stories flowed from him. It was like stepping back into history, listening to his tales of the independence movement, his early days working with Gandhi, and the very special day, 15 August 1947, when Manibhai watched the flag of an independent India go up the flagpole for the first time. As he watched it rise, he took an oath that he would never marry, but would instead dedicate his entire life to improving the lives of the rural poor.

His extraordinary success was evident in every area he ventured into. When he discovered the poor production capabilities of the indigenous Indian dairy cow, he began to research crossbreeding. By the time he had completed his research, milk production was increased over six-fold, and to this day—decades later—crossbreeding and distribution of semen from these crossbred cows are done nationally.

When he saw the subabul tree on a trip to Hawaii, Manibhai returned with just a handful of seeds. That handful eventually became hundreds of thousands of what are now called "miracle trees," for every part can be used, they grow tall rapidly, and, when you cut them down, they come back again!

As his work evolved and broadened, Manibhai's philosophy also developed. When he talked about the rural people who were poor and mostly uneducated, his understanding and respect for them was obvious in statements like, "Yes, maybe they don't take a bath, but remember they don't have water. . . ."

As we talked, it became clear that, from the very beginning, Manibhai had not just stood back and ordered others around. When a well needed digging, he picked up the shovel and began digging. He was then quickly joined by other men in the village.

When he was working with a village, he didn't go in, look around, and tell them what they needed. Instead, he and the villagers together determined what they needed and how to get it. He called this the "bottom up" philosophy.

As we spent more time together, I realized that I admired, respected, and dearly loved this gentle, unassuming man. He had a sense of humor, a sense of dedication, a determination, and a recognizable goal always in front of him. He had not only become an Earth Angel in my life but was a human angel shared by a nation and much of the world.

Gandhi had originally placed him in charge of a single ashram that eventually grew into BAIF and was organized as a national nonprofit organization in 1967. Manibhai was presented with innumerable awards yet, as he and his organization became more successful and nationally recognized, he never lost sight of the fact that his purpose was not to reap rewards, but to improve the quality of life for those in need.

In 1993 when I was visiting India to make a video, I went to Pune and interviewed Manibhai. For over an hour we sat on a bench in a garden area and talked, while the cameraman focused on him and his responses to my questions. When we were finished, I said, "Oh, thank you so much for all your help." Manibhai then paid me the nicest compliment I have ever received. He took my hand and said, "No, no, Connie, we don't thank each other for doing our job. You are one of us and we are all simply doing our job." These were the last words Manibhai spoke to me. The following November he died quietly in his sleep.

But it was during that last visit that I learned the most important lesson of my life and one that I believe will live with me forever. Like so many people, I had always assumed that fame and fortune were the most important goals in life. But that day, as Manibhai walked through the village for our meeting, he strolled along smiling at everyone, and I saw the faces of the people as they saw him approach. I realized, at that moment, that all the fame and fortune in the world could not replace the expressions of caring on the faces of these villagers. Though he had raised billions for rural development projects, had won dozens of awards, and was internationally acknowledged for his humanity, the expressions on these faces revealed the real fame and fortune of Manibhai Desai.

When I give my talks about Manibhai and his work, I always conclude with: "The greatest gift I ever received in my lifetime was the gift of friendship I received from Manibhai Desai. Along with the millions whose lives were improved by his work, I, too, have had my life touched and blessed by knowing him. I wish that each of you will someday know the true joy of having a Manibhai Desai in your life."

Jason, the Invincible

Susan Wright • 43 • Owner, Secretarial Service

My Earth Angel, Jason, was born on December 11, 1973. At the age of three-and-a-half he was diagnosed with a cancerous brain stem tumor. At the time, it was the fifth largest killer of children. I remember the doctors saying that he would probably be gone in six months. I went home and marked the last day of that sixth month on the calendar, not out of resignation, but as a way of trying to face reality.

Then my son, Jason, and I began the fight. Radiation and chemotherapy were still in the testing stages and there were terrible side effects. Jason's grandmother gave him a Superman outfit to help him feel better, and after the chemotherapy, he would run down the halls in his cape while all the other children were vomiting. He believed he could become a super hero and conquer the cancer. My mom called him "Jason, the invincible."

The children would watch Jason run around the hospital with his bright red Superman cape flying behind him, and their faces would light up. If only for that moment, the children forgot their pain, and their spirits were lifted. I began to notice Jason's effect on people even though he was so young. His positive attitude inspired and gave strength to everyone around him.

Jason was always aware of his surroundings and could tell when something wasn't right. At times I felt as if he could see into me. He would look up at me and say, "Don't worry, Mommy," at the exact moment I needed to hear those words. Then he would say, "If bullets can't hurt Superman, then this can't hurt me."

Remarkably, he was right. Jason's tumor calcified and no longer threatened his health. It was, in a sense, a miracle. Out of eighty-two children, Jason became the only survivor. Children's Hospital in Los Angeles asked him to be their poster child. And so he became an inspiration, not only to the people he met, but to the people who saw his picture and read his story.

Unfortunately that was not the end of Jason's troubles. The chemotherapy and radiation had left his lungs in bad shape, and we spent the next fourteen years trying to repair the damage.

I remember days and nights at Children's Hospital sleeping under Jason's crib. There was no place else for me to sleep, and I wasn't going to leave my child. On many nights I was awakened by the janitor's broom.

Because of this experience, Jason and I helped start the Ronald McDonald House. Parents sometimes have to travel far to get the best treatment for their kids, and they usually need a place to stay. The Ronald McDonald House provides affordable lodging—not to mention great French fries.

Being the parent of an ill child can be very lonely at times. Being in an environment where others are experiencing similar feelings helps lessen the loneliness. Jason was a great spokesperson for the Ronald McDonald House and we would often go there to visit. While I talked with the parents, Jason entertained the kids.

Everywhere Jason went, he lit up the room. He talked to the children who were still suffering through treatments and told them that if he could do it, they could too.

In high school Jason wanted to play basketball, but he was too short. He only grew to three-feet-eleven inches because the treatments had stunted his growth. But that didn't stop "Jason, the invincible." He decided that if he couldn't play basketball, he would surround himself with basketball. They made him team manager and you could tell he was their inspiration. He helped motivate the boys. My little guy was as big as they were when it came to will. If he noticed that their spirits were down during a game, he would say, "Never give up!" It was like injecting those kids with his own strength, and then they would be back on the court, stronger than ever.

When we found out that Jason needed a lung transplant, we began our search for a donor. Though several family members, friends, and I offered, the doctors didn't want to take part of a lung from someone healthy. We needed a donor. It was a battle I hadn't known we would need to fight.

I dragged Jason and his oxygen tank straight down to the organization that matches the donor lists to the lists of people who need transplants. I felt it might make a difference if they met Jason instead of just seeing a name on a list.

We walked into an office full of people talking and computer screens flickering. It was during their lunch and some of the people were standing around eating pizza. I stood there, not knowing exactly whom to talk to, but Jason spoke up: "Smells like a new pair of lungs. Got any?" We were all surprised, and then everybody smiled. A few minutes after Jason introduced himself, we were inside the president's office.

That was when I realized that people needed to meet Jason, that he couldn't be some faceless name. I also felt that if Jason's story were publicized, others in his predicament would also benefit. We wanted to help educate the public on becoming a donor. We wanted to dispel the myth that a loved one who became a donor would be disfigured. (Donor operations are treated with the same respect as live operations.)

Channel 7 news in Los Angeles did a story on Jason. I remember one of the news anchors choking up and having to turn the story over to another anchor.

Jason and his story affected people. He brought them into his world and showed them that there was nothing to be afraid of. He helped promote Donor Awareness Week and, in his frail state, he even put up posters.

Jason had the opportunity to flex his muscles with Hulk Hogan during the three hours he spent at our home. In addition to this large and lovely man, Jason had a lot of Earth Angels trying to help.

Finally one of the doctors came through; they had found lungs for Jason.

As Jason was being wheeled into the operating room, he said,

"I love to see all of my people gathered in one place." Everyone smiled.

Jason was lying on the operating table, prepped and ready. We were told that the donor was a five-year-old and that the heart was going to a seven-year-old girl in the operating room next door. I stood there waiting, with Jason's hand in mine, when a young doctor came into the room.

"I'm so sorry, Jason," he said, as the tears welled up in his eyes, "the lungs were too badly damaged." The doctor turned away from us, trying not to show his emotion. "I'm sorry," he repeated.

I felt as if the room had caved in on me. Jason squeezed my hand and looked at the doctor. "Is the heart a go?" he asked.

The doctor quickly turned and looked at Jason. "Yes," he answered.

I'll never forget Jason's generous smile at that moment. Everyone in the operating room shifted from feeling profound disappointment to thinking about the little girl who would get a heart.

It is difficult to describe what we went through waiting for a donor. Jason's lung capacity had diminished to only 15 percent. It was so low that it didn't register on the computer. At twenty-two years old, he needed a double lung transplant in order to survive.

He kept reassuring me. "One day they're going to find just the right lungs for me," he would say, taking a breath between each word. Then he'd smile.

That day finally came. They had found a donor. Jason was finally going to get new lungs!

There was just one problem. Jason had lost most of his sight from, I believed, the medication he was taking. In order to accept a transplant, the patient must be in otherwise good health. I knew that if they learned Jason's sight was almost gone, they wouldn't go ahead with the transplant.

Jason fooled them all. He walked right up to the doctors and even shook their hands. I tried my best not to appear surprised. When they were wheeling him into the operating room, he looked up at me and said, "This is what I dreamed of. This is my happiest moment."

"Just come back to me," I said.

I sat in the waiting room impatiently, with my family and about thirty strangers. I found out that the donor was another five-year-old who had died and that the three families in the room were waiting for the heart, the liver, and Jason's new lungs.

My son, Jason Pittman, lived for twelve hours after the surgery; the lung transplant had been a success, but Jason died of a heart attack.

What Jason did in his twenty-two years was an accomplishment of a lifetime. He touched and inspired people. He took away the fear people have of someone being different.

A few days after he was gone, I was having my car fixed. My mechanic asked about Jason (we had always been together), and I told him Jason had died. This large, gruff man had tears in his eyes. He said, "I became an organ donor because of Jason."

"Thank you," I said. I realized that Jason had done his work on earth.

At his funeral in November 1996, over five hundred people came to pay tribute to this special human being.

My husband and I were invited to a basketball game at Jason's old high school two weeks after his funeral. I forced myself to go, or rather, I was coerced by the coach. When we arrived, we were surprised to see that all the team members were wearing "First Annual Jason Pittman Alumni Game" T-shirts. The coach made a speech saying, "The thing I remember most about Jason was him carrying the team jackets. All you could see were his tennis shoes."

Recently, on a rainy day, I felt really down. I missed Jason terribly. I didn't even want to leave the house. So I decided to get the mail. (Since the funeral, cards and letters had been flooding the mailbox, mostly with letters from strangers who talked about Jason as if he were their good friend. I continue to receive letters even today.)

It had begun to rain harder, and I knew that if I didn't get the mail soon, the overflow, which was left on top of the mailbox, would be ruined. So I hurried down the driveway.

While thumbing through the beautifully colored envelopes, I came across one that said CONGRATULATIONS on the front. I opened it to find a letter from Robitussin informing me that I was a finalist in their "Mother of the Year" contest. Jason had never told me, and once again he had brightened my day.

Every day, in one way or another, my Earth Angel, Jason, comes back to me.

Chapter 7

Miracles

No one really knows where miracles come from.
Some people believe they come from the shimmering stars.
Others think they are found only in fanciful fairy tales.
The fact is, the universe is full of miracles.
They are all around us.
However, you must believe in miracles if you hope to see them.
A day will come when YOU meet a miracle—
And your world will never be the same.
Perhaps that day is today . . .

> —*From* The Midnight Miracle,
> by Jerry Biederman and Christopher Owens

Regardless of who we are, our lives are blessed with miracles. When a child is born we are able to bear witness to the miracle of life. When, against all odds, someone survives a plane crash, we wonder if this miracle is the result of divine intervention. And every day many of us are lucky enough to experience small but significant miracles—when someone finds their true love after they had almost lost hope; when a struggling actor gets selected for a role among the hundreds who auditioned; when the smallest boy on the team hits a home run; when you find a parking space at the mall on the day before Christmas.

This final chapter is a collection of stories that show how miracles can come to us at any time and how they are often delivered by an Earth Angel.

We heard a miraculous story over the phone one day when we returned a mysterious call on our Earth Angels hotline. An Irishman had left the number of a pay phone somewhere in San Francisco, along with an exact time and day to reach him.

When we called, the Irishman was there, as he had promised. He said he had read about our search in a newspaper article and felt compelled to call.

We spoke intensely for fifteen minutes, until he said he had to go. We still needed information to complete his story, so we asked when we could arrange to speak again. It was decided that our next call would be to the same pay phone at exactly noon the following day.

The phone rang and rang before it was finally answered. But it was not the Irishman. A stranger's voice said there was no one else around and hung up. Although we tried calling that same number *minutes later, and then at different times throughout that day and the next, we never spoke again.*

The man seemed to be a lost soul with a miraculous story . . .

Golden Gate

Patrick • 38 • Unknown

It is said that angels come when we need them most.

I'm from a small village in Ireland, and I come from an upstanding and well-respected family. I had spent all my life in this safe and secure haven, and it was here that I met my true love. Melissa had moved into town with her parents two years before, and I knew, when our eyes first met, that she was the one.

We were engaged and planning our wedding when Melissa asked if she could come over one evening (less than a month from our sacred date). I was thrilled to see her shining eyes, but I saw that something was wrong. I don't recall all that she said. All I know is that she broke our engagement along with my heart, and walked out the door.

I did not want to live without Melissa, and, if God wouldn't set me free, I would have to take matters into my own hands.

There was no way I could dishonor my family. If they, or anyone else, found out I had taken my life, my family would suffer from shame.

I remembered reading an article once that said the most common place and time to commit such an act was on the Golden Gate Bridge on a Monday.

I hugged my parents and told them I was going for a walk. I tried not to weep until I was far down the road.

When I arrived in San Francisco late Sunday afternoon, I discarded all my personal identification, including my passport, in a receptacle. My parents would never know it was I who had jumped off the bridge that Monday. Instead I would be a John Doe, nameless and free.

Not having anywhere to sleep, I wandered the streets, up and down the hills, until I saw the sun rising over the beautiful city and shining on the bridge.

A large sign sparkled above me; it read: "Golden Gate Bridge." The wind was cold and seemed to push me on and, the next thing I knew, I was high above the bay looking out across the water.

Melissa's face rushed into my head and her words, "I have to go," squeezed my heart with a fury.

I put my hands on the railing and was about to lift myself over, when I felt a hand on my shoulder.

"Patrick. That you?" I heard the familiar voice say.

I turned around to find the face of Brian McGee, a childhood friend from my village in Ireland.

"Plannin' on jumpin' in, old friend?" he laughed.

I laughed too (a nervous laugh).

For some reason my life was spared. It was a miracle. Without his knowing, Brian was the angel sent to save me.

Although I don't know what tomorrow shall bring, I now believe that there is an important reason I am still here. Perhaps I am on earth to be an angel in someone else's life. I guess my story is still being written.

Through the Woods

Dee Anne • 34 • Stock Broker

I haven't told this story to anyone since the day it happened. I was very young when it took place, and I was sure no one would believe me.

When I was a little girl, I had to skirt a large park filled with trees and shrubs each day on my way to school. I wasn't allowed to walk through the park even though it would have been much faster. My parents were afraid that God-knows-what might happen to a little girl walking through the woods alone.

One day I was very late leaving school, and I wanted to get

home before my mother started worrying. I decided to take a shortcut through the park in an effort to save some time, but I didn't know the way, and, when I finally made it through the woods, I was lost. None of the streets or houses looked familiar; I didn't recognize a thing.

Not knowing what else to do, I started wandering around, hoping that I would see something familiar. It was getting late, the sun was setting, and I was becoming more lost and afraid.

I had just started to cry when I saw an old man coming down the street toward me. He was kind and gentle-looking, and he stopped to ask why I was crying.

I told him that I was lost and that my Nanie (that's what I called my grandmother) and mother would be worried.

He smiled at me and told me not to cry, saying that he knew my Nanie very well. He said his name was Charlie.

He took my hand and walked me home, which turned out to be only a few blocks away. I was so excited to recognize my street that when my house finally came into view, I ran toward it in joyful relief. I looked back once to see if Charlie was coming—but he was gone.

I told my mother I had been lost and that Nanie's friend had brought me home. When I told her his name she seemed puzzled. She said she didn't know anyone in the neighborhood named Charlie. She mentioned that my grandfather's name was Charlie, but that he had been dead for years, and with that, she forgot all about it.

Her mention of my grandfather started me thinking, though.

I remembered how I had looked back to see him, and how he had mysteriously disappeared.

I know that it seems ridiculous, but I can't shake the feeling that the old man *was* my grandfather Charlie bringing me safely home.

I think he was sent down from heaven that day, to be my Earth Angel.

The Greatest Gift

Ginger L. Morgan • *31* • *Public Relations Practitioner*

This past holiday season, I couldn't help but notice how different my life is than it was last year at this time.

It was December, one year ago, and, like many married couples, my husband and I awoke, showered, dressed, kissed, and drove in different directions to our office jobs. Nine hours later we returned, dropped our briefcases, and ate dinner on trays in front of the television, like two teens with vacationing parents. But something was missing.

Happy with our new marriage, we were almost ready for the next step—children. In our courtship days, we had decided we would eventually adopt, since I've been diabetic all my life. Bearing our own biological children didn't seem worth the risk to my body and, more important, to our baby. Since we figured adoption could take a while, we decided to start right away.

We put a call in to our attorney, casually informing him, "Sometime next year would be good. We're in no hurry."

Three months later I took a one-week vacation and flew to Colorado with my husband. It was the day before Christmas Eve and we were standing in my parents' kitchen when the phone rang. Our attorney had tracked us down.

"I know it's sooner than you had anticipated," we heard over the telephone, "but we have a two-day-old girl who needs a home. Do you want her?"

We were numb with shock, but as we stood in that kitchen looking at each other, we knew our answer—"Yes." Our attorney instructed us to call the birth mother, arrange a meeting place in her city, and drive there as quickly as we could.

We planned to meet at a restaurant near her home. If she considered us suitable parents, we could have the baby. Meeting the mother was, in itself, a growth experience; nobody prepares you for this situation. How do you behave when the most wonderful event of your life—becoming a parent—results in an agonizing loss for someone else?

You just answer her questions and hope for a miracle.

Apparently satisfied with our answers, this twenty-one-year-old mother of two agreed to give us the greatest gift we had ever received. Yet we couldn't allow ourselves to be elated as we watched her hug her baby, feed her for the last time, and tearfully admonish us to watch for milk allergy.

It took all my strength not to cry as she placed the little bundle in my arms. For a moment our eyes locked, and we both seemed to understand what the other was feeling. "Thank you," I whispered.

"Please tell her I loved her." She could barely get the words out as she quickly wiped a tear from her cheek and turned away.

"I promise," I told her.

I wonder what my husband and I looked like, walking out of that restaurant with a baby we hadn't brought in. I wonder if we looked as dreadfully nervous as we felt. I don't think I looked up once on our way to the car. I couldn't take my eyes off this sleeping child—our daughter.

It seemed fateful that a Wal-Mart, the uniquely American bastion of—well—everything was just across the street.

"Nipples, bottles, formula, diapers, wipes!" I shotgunned at my husband, whose throat was as tight as mine. Glad to have a few moments alone to gather his thoughts, he disappeared into the store.

Pulling into our driveway at two o'clock in the morning, we jumped out. Anxious to check her diaper, at that point a two-person job, my husband left the car running.

The night turned into a Keystone Kops routine as we changed our first diaper:

"Where do the tabs go?"

"In the back. Aren't we supposed to put powder on her?"

"Powder? We don't have any. Would flour work?"

And so on.

Having no crib, we lined a laundry basket with towels. Catherine hated it, so she slept on top of me—and I loved it.

When we awoke from our nonsleep, my husband frowned: something was wrong. How could something be wrong? It was Christmas Eve morning and we had the most beautiful baby girl.

"What's wrong?" I asked, kissing Catherine's forehead and then his.

"I left the car running in the driveway all night." We both laughed as he ran out with his robe half off one shoulder.

Later that day, I called work and told them I had had a great vacation and that, by the way, "I'm a mom." And realizing, at that moment, how important my *new job* was, I decided to quit the old one.

And now, instead of worrying about employee evaluations and how to find appropriate photos for the October issue of the magazine, my concerns center around soy formula, DTP inoculations, and cleaning food from the walls. I power lunch with someone in a bib. My husband watches NASCAR races with a new pretty girl, his one-year-old daughter.

Talk about a sudden leap in quality of life. I guess miracles happen quickly.

Produced by a tall, thin, black man, and a white woman who happens to look a lot like me, Catherine attracts compliments wherever we go.

"What a beautiful baby! What's her heritage?"

"Where did she get that incredible hair?"

"Those eyes! They're huge!"

Catherine is our Earth Angel. Anyone who knows what it's like to hold a baby in their arms knows what heaven feels like. Catherine has brought heaven to earth for us and we will always be grateful to her birth mother, whom I think about a lot; I remember how difficult it was to take Catherine from her. The best day of our lives was the worst day of hers.

Since that day she has written three long letters to Catherine explaining why she made the decision to give her up and how very much she loves her. Because of her letters, we will never have to explain to our daughter why someone didn't want her, because she *was* wanted. Her birth mother decided to give her daughter the gift of a better life. It was a more loving thing to do than keeping her would have been.

She didn't give away a child; she created a miracle and gave two strangers the greatest gift imaginable.

Who Needs Bells?

Donna Schaper • *50* • *Ordained Minister*

A well-meaning member of my former church in New York showed up one day to donate bells.

"Bells? Who needs bells?" was my first reaction. "Didn't you see the line for the soup kitchen at lunch? Don't you know that we have homeless people here who need food?" *Bells were the last thing we needed*, I thought.

She took me with that proverbial grain of salt that many parishioners use on their pastors, and donated the bells anyway. Before we knew it, the bells were ringing out of our church steeple at eight o'clock, noon, and five o'clock.

I noticed that the soup kitchen line had a little more life in its step.

One night at a church meeting, the director of the local battered women's shelter said to me with tears in her eyes, "I was walking home last night and I heard your bells. It had been a terrible day and I was so grateful for the music."

All my doubts melted that night.

Those who battle real hunger, disease, and violence deserve music to battle by. Bells give that kind of music. It is the music that fountain water dances to—the music of the unnecessary, the discipline beyond the daily discipline, the lyric that we live by more than bread alone. Music is nourishment for the heart.

Light, water, music. Let's dance—then we'll eat.

The Magic Christmas

Cheryl Wenzel • 40 • Small Business Owner

I thought you might like to hear a story about the Christmas when I discovered that there really is a Santa.

I'm going to tell it without too many of the gory details, but I have to set it up a little, so that you can grasp how things were when all this happened:

The world I had lived in for thirteen years came to an abrupt halt on October thirtieth. During those years of marriage, I had been emotionally and sometimes physically abused. That day, the physical abuse went too far, and by the time he left, some days later, I was just grateful to be alive.

He must have been planning to leave for a while because one day, when I wasn't home, he cleaned the place out. You wouldn't believe how much three men can move in one afternoon, when the motivation is greed.

There wasn't any money in the bank because the accounts

had been closed, and he even took the money out of the kids' savings accounts. How was I going to take care of four children and a fifth on the way? I didn't have a job, and there was no financial support because there wasn't a court order yet. The kids helped me break open their piggy banks, and I dug into the couches and chairs to find what I could. Pretty slim picking, to say the least.

So, as you can tell, I didn't know where I would get the next dollar. I sold anything I could just to get the money to pay the rent and buy food.

Okay, that's a little background, and now, here's the story of the magic . . .

With all that was going on and going wrong, when my birthday came around, I made a wish on the full moon. I wished that I would be able to give my kids a Christmas. All I could do was make wishes.

It didn't look very promising. I didn't have the money for a tree or gifts. My husband had taken the decorations he wanted and destroyed the rest. I wouldn't even be able to give them a special Christmas dinner; there sure wouldn't be a turkey.

But it didn't matter what I had to do, because I would find the money to get something from Santa.

I had an idea about how I could bring at least a part of Christmas to them. If I went to the tree lot and asked for the bows they trim from the trees, I could make a wreath. And if I could get enough bows, I would weave them into something resembling a tree. It might only be a foot tall and sit on the kitchen table, but the size wouldn't matter.

I tried to make it an adventure for the kids and told them what we were going to do. So by the time we got to the lot, they were pretty excited about helping mommy make a tree.

I asked the men for the trimmings, telling them I wanted to make a little wreath for the door. (My pride was about all I had left, and I couldn't bring myself to tell them the truth.) They said I could have all I wanted, to help myself. While my oldest daughter and I searched the grounds for the best branches, my son Matt, not quite four, wandered off. While he roamed among the giant trees, one of the men asked him what Santa was going to bring him. In the way only a little child can, he told the man that he didn't think Santa would find him this year because we wouldn't have a real tree.

As I finished loading the branches into the back of the truck, I called for Matt and told him it was time to go home. The man came up to me and, with tears in his eyes, told me he wanted us to pick out the best tree on the lot. He said he wanted me to have a tree for the kids so that Santa could find that little boy.

I didn't know what to say other than, "Thank you." I had to let the kids pick out the tree because I couldn't see through the grateful tears in my eyes. It wasn't until later that Matt told me what he had shared with the man. The men tied the tree onto the truck and we went home. I had to unload it and get it into the house, but when a neighbor saw that I didn't have help, he took over. He even set it up in the stand.

I found a little box of decorations that my husband had missed, and the kids and I made a lot of little snowflakes out of paper. The tree looked quite good given what we had to work with. And now the big question—where was I going to find the money to put something under it?

I took the kids to K-mart and let them look at the toys, hoping they would be able to find something they liked that I would be able to afford. I told them to pick a toy that they would like Santa to bring them and to close their eyes and make their Christmas wish. They chose such simple things that it amazed me.

I had a neighbor sit with them, and I went back to K-mart and put the things they had chosen on layaway until December twenty-fourth. I knew that somehow I would be able to get the money—$149.85—for the gifts.

A couple of weeks later, my mother called. She said that instead of buying the kids gifts that year, she and Dad thought they would just send a check. She said that, because they were so far away, it was too hard for them to buy just the right things. Though she didn't come out and say it, she knew how much we needed the money.

I was elated when she said she wanted to send $150. Perfect! I had the toy bill covered. I told her what I was going to do with the money and she cried. Then I told her about the tree and I cried.

Now the kids had a tree and some gifts for underneath it. The only thing left was to find something for Christmas dinner.

When the check came, I went to the store to pick up the toys. There was a drawing at the door. You put your name in the box and, throughout the day, they would call out names. If you were in the store shopping when your name was called, you won a turkey. I figured, what the heck. I wouldn't be there for very long, but I put my name in anyway. I was in the store for about three minutes, when I heard my name over the loud speaker! Well, now we had our turkey.

On the way home I went to the grocery store to buy some milk. They had the same type of drawing and, you guessed it—I won another turkey! During the next week, I entered drawings in other stores, and I ended up winning six turkeys! Okay, so at least we would have turkey for dinner.

Then one evening, shortly after winning the turkeys, I found a big box on the porch. There was no note and I didn't have any idea where it had come from. Inside was everything we needed to make our Christmas dinner complete: yams, baked beans, stuffing mix, instant pudding, pie shells, canned cherries, and, of course, a turkey.

A couple of days later, about a week before Christmas, I got a phone call. A lady whom I didn't know told me that her mother had passed away a couple of months earlier and that she had some of her tree decorations. She couldn't bear to put them on her tree and wanted to know if we could use them. I was shocked by her generosity and had no idea how she knew me or how she had gotten my phone number. Of course we could use the decorations, so I accepted and told her I would take care of them. Now we would even have lights for the tree!

She came the next day with the decorations. I invited her in for coffee, but she said she couldn't stay. Then she asked her husband to bring in another box. I had no idea what it was, and she told me not to open it until after they had left. I put the box in the kitchen and when I returned to the front door to thank her, ask her her name, and find out where she was from, she was already in the car, driving away.

I opened the box to find all kinds of toys and stuffed animals for the kids! There was also a small wrapped gift with my name on it. She had even put in a little stuffed lamb that played a tune, for the baby who was coming in the spring.

I didn't know who she was and I was never able to find out, hard as I tried. She may have been from a nearby church and could have heard about my situation from one of the neighbors. I asked around, but no one seemed to know.

Christmas morning was wonderful. Better than what I could have wished for.

The gift with my name on it was a silver apple. Of all the other things I have, it's my most special treasure.

The decorations are worn and old, but they go on the tree each Christmas just the same. My daughter still has the little lamb, and she asks me every year to tell her the story of *The Magic Christmas* before she was born. She knows the part about the lamb by heart. While its little fuzz is loved off in places, she sleeps with it nearby every night.

I am now remarried to a kind and gentle man. We had a child together and he has been a great father to all the children.

This year there is a full moon on Christmas Eve. You can be sure that I will bundle up, walk outside, look at the stars, and make another wish. I don't need one for myself this time. My life is more wonderful now than I had thought possible.

I only hope that Earth Angels find their way to others in need, as I was that special year when I received so much human kindness and learned to believe in the magic of wishes.

As Grand as Mozart

J. B. Nicholas • *29* • *Teacher*

I sat down to play my piano today and I thought of her. I don't remember the first time I met Ms. Julia Robins, but my dad tells me we were instant friends.

I do remember how Raleigh looked at Christmastime. It was the only house we knew that had a name. Dad drove through the tall, iron gates and we all marveled at the snow-covered grounds with twinkling lights in the trees. My brother, my sister, and I always fought over who got to ring the doorbell. We anticipated the first glimpse of that enormous Christmas tree in the foyer before the door would open.

For us, Raleigh was magical. The parlor spoke of foreign lands, great writers, and comfortable gatherings. A dish of chocolates and peppermints always sat on the coffee table. After enduring grown-up talk for what seemed like hours, we were rewarded with tall parfaits—chocolate and vanilla ice cream and orange sherbet layered in frosted glasses with chilly, long spoons. We were treated like kings and queens.

After a while Ms. Robins would suggest we have a little music. We'd march downstairs to the basement and everyone would settle into overstuffed couches. I'd adjust the piano bench and run my fingers along the ivory keys. Her piano was always in perfect condition and I couldn't wait to hear the beautiful sounds it resonated. I played my holiday repertoire amidst the hushed tones of conversation. As a piece ended, there would be ecstatic clapping, especially from her. "Isn't she precious?" I'd hear her whisper, and I felt as grand as Mozart.

On my sixteenth birthday my parents surprised me by taking me to Kitts-Jordan to pick out a piano. I was overwhelmed. I didn't think twice about how my parents would afford it, all I could think about was that I would have a piano of my own. I remember searching the store with Mom and Dad until I saw the perfect one.

My parents wrote down the model number of the piano and we started to walk out of the store.

"Where are we going?" I asked.

"Ms. Robins is going to take care of the rest," my father said with a smile. I think I was too young to realize the magnitude of Ms. Robins's generosity.

The day the piano arrived I could hardly contain my excitement. Some men from church unpacked it and I watched them place it carefully against the living room wall. When they were finished I sat down and stared at my reflection in the glossy finish. Anxious to play, I put my hands on the beautifully lacquered keys.

"J. B.," I heard my mother's voice, "shouldn't you write that thank-you note before you do anything else?"

I sat in a chair next to the piano and began to write a note. I wanted to write something special to thank Ms. Robins for this beautiful and generous gift.

Several weeks later, my mother told me we were having a special visitor.

"Who?" I asked.

"You'll see," my mother replied.

The doorbell rang and I ran to answer it—curious as to whom this mysterious visitor was. I opened the door and was so surprised to see Ms. Robins standing there.

"Hi, J. B.," she said in her raspy voice. "I came to watch you play your new piano. May I come in?"

"Oh yes," I said—a little embarrassed for not asking her to come in right away.

We all sat in the living room around the piano. My father made sure Ms. Robins had the comfortable chair closest to me. When I finished the sonata I heard her whisper, "Isn't she precious?"

We continued to visit Ms. Robins at Raleigh. Sometimes we came in shifts due to busy high school schedules. But she was always gracious and understanding. There was still the grown-up talk, but now questions like, "Where are you thinking of going to college?" filtered into the conversation. I wasn't sure if I would be able to go because finances were tight. My piano playing improved and the pieces were longer and filled with runs and trills. She would always whisper, "Isn't she precious?" I feigned disinterest but deep inside I felt as grand as Mozart.

In my senior year of high school my mom and dad told me to apply to the college of my choice. Before I could even ask how we would afford it, they said that it was important for my future and they would manage. I remember how excited Ms. Robins was that I chose Wheaton College in Illinois. Though she had never attended, she had much respect for the college. "Billy Graham went there," she said proudly.

The four years at Wheaton seemed to go by so quickly. After graduation I stayed on in Wheaton for the summer. I wrote my parents a note telling them how much I appreciated their making sacrifices so that I could go to college.

A few days later Dad called. "J. B., we loved your note. We wanted to tell you that we have always done what we could, but we can't take all of the credit. Just after you left for college we received a check in the mail. It was from Ms. Robins and it was for the exact amount of your tuition. The checks have been coming ever since and they seem to arrive just before tuition is due. We tried to thank her but you know Ms. Robins. She just shushed us and told us she never wanted to hear a thing about it. It was her pleasure."

The lump in my throat rendered me speechless and I couldn't hold back the tears. She had given me a gift that would last my lifetime and made a dream of mine come true. I wished that I could somehow repay her for her kindness. "I . . ."

"We know how you feel, honey," my dad continued. "Ms. Julia Robins is our Earth Angel. Her generosity is like a gift from heaven—wonderful, complete, unconditional, and always a surprise."

Later, I married and my husband and I rented an apartment in Cincinnati. We were going to drive the three hundred miles with most of our belongings, but the piano had to be shipped. My parents said they would split the cost with us. I remember walking into our empty apartment and seeing the only piece of furniture sitting where I had left the note for the movers. For the first time I realized that the piano was really mine and my piano seemed to welcome us home. I wished I could have run down the street to Raleigh and put my arms around Ms. Robins. Instead, I brushed off the bench, sat down, and played one of her favorite sonatas.

I want to thank Ms. Julia Robins for believing in me and my family. When I visited her last Christmas her memory was fading because she is now in her nineties, and it took a few moments for her to recognize me. I read a letter I had written telling her that she was my Earth Angel. When I was finished she looked up at my father and whispered, "Isn't she precious?"

As I left, I stood for a moment in front of Raleigh not knowing if I'd ever return. It was magical. The Christmas tree still towered over the foyer, and in my mind I could still taste the sweet parfaits fit for royalty.

When I sat down to play my piano today I thought of my Earth Angel and I felt as grand as Mozart.

Don't Sit By

Christi Ball • 14 • Hobbies: Tennis and Horseback Riding

My Earth Angel showed me how to see the good in the world and she taught me the importance of standing up for what is right.

It seems as though she was born to fight injustice. At the age of twenty-four she happened to be living at a time and place in the world's history known for its injustice. It was World War II and she was in German-occupied Poland.

She lived with her family in a town called Poznan. She had three brothers and two sisters. They were a Catholic family. Her father was a baker. And she became a spy.

This lady-spy was petite, with wavy brunette hair, blue-green eyes, and a contagious laugh. She was beautiful, intelligent, selfless, and, as it turned out, very courageous. Her name was Janina. It's rare to find such a soul who would not compromise between right and wrong, even if it meant her own life would be placed in peril.

Janina joined the underground against Nazi Germany because she couldn't bear the injustices that were happening to innocent people all around her. She would witness the atrocities whenever she would visit the labor camps with her mother. They were volunteers who helped feed the prisoners. Since Janina was a nurse, she tended to the sick and injured.

As the Nazi horrors grew, Janina couldn't take it any longer. She felt she had to act against the Nazis, and that was when she joined the allied underground. Every Monday she would go to an evening mass, sit at the second pew from the back, open up the missalette, and find notes from other members of the underground telling her when and where they were to assemble for their secret meetings. Risking her own life, Janina distributed anti-Nazi propaganda and disseminated broadcasts in Poland from England and Radio Free Europe.

But there was a leak! Someone told the Gestapo about the group of spies. In November of 1942, in the middle of the night, the Gestapo came pounding on the door of Janina's house. They barged in and took her away at gunpoint. Her father couldn't stop them or else the whole family would have been killed.

Janina's family didn't know what had hit them. They didn't know why the Gestapo had come to *their* home and why Janina had been the target of their assault. In order to protect her family, Janina had made sure no one in her family knew. She had kept it a secret even from her sister, Vanda, who was her very best friend.

For a year her family didn't know if she was dead or alive. Vanda was quite brave and went down to Gestapo headquarters to pursue what had happened to her sister. She discovered that Janina had been shipped off to a concentration camp called Auschwitz.

What the Gestapo didn't reveal, however, was that before

Janina went to Auschwitz, she spent six months in a top secret site known as Fort 7. It was a place for interrogation and torture. What occurred there was so horrible that Janina never spoke fully of her experiences.

At Auschwitz she wore a large "P" across her chest. It stood for "political prisoner." Since she was trained as a nurse, the Nazis put her to work in the ambulatory ward of the camp. There, she helped the sick and the dying prisoners. Even though she was, herself, severely malnourished and sick with typhus, she gave everything she could to the other prisoners.

Janina saved many lives in Auschwitz. Every day the camp guards made their inspections of the sick prisoners. The ones who appeared near death were taken out and killed. Janina would run ahead of the guards to the most severely ill prisoners and pinch their cheeks so hard that they turned to a rosy pink. So, when the guards came, they would not kill these prisoners because their rosy cheeks made them appear healthy.

Remarkably, Janina escaped Auschwitz. It was a fall night in 1944. Janina was part of a group of prisoners being temporarily transported outside the concentration camp. She and a prisoner friend jumped off the train and disappeared into a cornfield. Running from their Nazi captors, she and her friend decided to split up because they knew they would have a better chance of getting caught if there were two of them. Janina made her way through Germany and eventually into occupied France. There, still in danger of being captured, she met a farmer who offered to hide her from the Nazis in his barn. The French farmer had a teenage daughter who was petrified, knowing that if the Germans discovered Janina, her family would be executed. A few days later everyone was relieved when American soldiers came through the town and arranged safe passage for Janina to England.

Once Janina reached her destination, she volunteered to be a nurse in the English army. She helped the badly wounded and wrote heartfelt letters to the parents of military men who had died.

After the war, Janina furthered her education and became a midwife. In the 1950s she immigrated to Canada. It was on the boat that she met her future husband. He was also from Poland. Once in Canada, she worked as a nurse specializing in obstetrics. There, they made a beautiful home and had a baby of their own.

That baby would one day grow up to become *my* mother. Yes, Janina was my grandmother.

I believe that Janina was an Earth Angel to the hundreds of innocent people she saved during World War II. But she became *my* Earth Angel, too.

I've always felt like I've had a special connection with her in a way that no one else did. Whenever I was around Granny she wouldn't have to speak and I would know what she was feeling.

I never heard her talk about her terrible time in the concentration camp. She shielded the family from it; I think her silence was her way of protecting us from the evil. She didn't look back—she lived for today. But during the summertime she couldn't escape the fact that she had been a prisoner in a Nazi concentration camp. On hot days, when she would wear short sleeves, people would ask her questions about the strange markings on her arm. Once someone asked, "Why is your phone number tattooed on your arm?" She could have very easily been nasty, but she realized that they didn't know. She simply said, "It's not my phone number," and just left it at that.

She cherished life and chose to see the good in the world. Not only did she not hold a grudge against the Nazis, but she felt sorry for them doing the things they did. She was very forgiving.

Granny taught me to never lose faith in humanity. Through her eyes I saw the bright side of life.

Although she put the war behind her, she never stopped fighting her battles against injustice. My mother told me about an incident when she and Granny were on a tour boat during one of their annual trips to Paris. A man was being abusive to his daughter, hitting her and yelling at her, and Granny came to the little girl's rescue.

She always said, "Don't sit by. You have to act."

The Nazis didn't get her, but cancer did. Granny died last March. My life has been a good one, in many ways thanks to Granny. I have many wonderful memories of my times with her. I will remember Granny by my favorite picture of her—she is standing in the middle of a rose garden, beautiful and happy.

My mother recently said something to me that made me feel so proud and even closer to Granny. There had been an incident at school. I noticed a bully was bothering this kid and I stepped in to help. When my mother heard about what had happened, she took my hand and said, "Christi, Granny lives inside of you. Like her, you can't just sit by when it comes to injustice."

It seems as though I was born to be her granddaughter. I will always love my Earth Angel and forever look up to her.

Before You Go

W̲e wanted to tell you, our reader, what a wonderful experience it was to write this book.

Writers are traditionally pictured alone in their studies, surrounded by books, a fireplace, and a window to dream out of. A lonely profession, indeed.

There was nothing lonely about writing *Earth Angels*. We had each other, and we had the thousands of people who came into our lives and shared themselves with us.

Usually we interviewed people at places such as a coffee shop, an office lunch room, a movie line, a county fair, a park, or a bus bench. Sometimes we were invited into a stranger's home.

Many strangers have become friends during our writing of this book. We realized this when, one night, we decided to lay out on our living room carpet the assortment of stories we had collected. We thought it would be valuable to get a view of all the different Earth Angels together as one. It was the first time that we had slowed our search long enough to see where we were and where we were headed. Looking at the story titles side by side, along with the familiar names of the storytellers, made us think about our writing journey. We had met such wonderful people on this great adventure, and we had gotten to know better the people we already knew.

We had met Michael Reiss (the man who owns the house where we are living) just once, when we signed the lease. One afternoon we had to call him because the washing machine was broken. He gave us the name of the plumber and, knowing that we were authors, he asked how our writing was going. We told him about *Earth Angels* and our search for stories. Without hesitation, he invited us to be his guests at a meeting of a neighborhood book club that he had founded. It was a fantastic evening. We met at a member's house, and all of us sat in a circle in front of the fireplace. Michael asked everyone to introduce themselves and to tell a little about why they loved books. Then, one by one, they went around the room telling their heartwarming stories. One older lady whispered to us that she was so excited that she might actually end up *in* a book. When everyone finished their stories, Michael shared a very personal one of his own ("The Wonderful World of Fiction"). At the end of the evening, as we were all getting up to leave, one woman asked another if she needed a ride. "Let me take you home," she said. "Let me be your Earth Angel." We all smiled. The spirit of *Earth Angels* had begun to spread!

In only a few months, our home became decorated with pictures that storytellers had sent to us of themselves, their families, and even their pets.

Ginger Morgan ("The Greatest Gift") sent us beautiful pictures of herself and her daughter, Catherine. We look at their smiling faces whenever we sit at our computer. We have been corresponding with them and hope to watch Catherine grow through the years.

There were more than three thousand kids from high schools and junior high schools who wrote Earth Angel stories. When we read them, they gave us so much hope for the future. Though many of the students touched us, one, in particular, found her way into our hearts.

One afternoon, we received an e-mail from Nicole Butolph, a teenager from a high school just outside of town. She wrote, "My Earth Angel taught me to always say thank you. I want to tell you that I never met adults who weren't too scared or preoccupied to listen to kids. It's kinda cool to know they exist. I was starting to wonder."

Since then, we have been corresponding with Nicole. We told her that, coincidentally, someday when we have kids, we'd like to name our daughter Nicole. Soon after, another e-mail arrived and at the end it read, "Nicole Biederman—sounds heavenly." What she isn't aware of is that we had a miscarriage a couple of years ago. Seeing this name on our computer screen renewed our hope for a Nicole of our own. When that day comes, there will be two Earth Angels in our lives named Nicole.

Along our journey, we very much wanted to see Earth Angels through the eyes of young children. We were invited to visit our niece's elementary school class at St. Mel School. The teacher, Heidi Detamore, said she would be happy to tell the kids about our book.

"They'll be so excited about sharing their stories," she told us, as we stood at her desk after class had let out.

A few weeks later, we returned to the school and met Heidi in her classroom. She handed us a folder filled with stories, each carefully printed on lined school paper. Just holding them felt good! We couldn't wait to read them, so we opened the folder and glanced at a couple of the stories. One entitled, "The Pizza Guy," immediately caught our eye. K. C. Croal wrote: "When I was five, I went for pizza with my mom at the mall. I ordered a cheese pizza but I told my mom I really wanted a lollipop. She just said, 'No!' The guy behind the counter heard her and handed me a purple lollipop. He smiled and said, 'It's on the house.' So the pizza guy is my Earth Angel."

We were laughing and walking out the door when a little

blond-haired boy flew in. In his hands was *his* Earth Angel story. He gave it to his teacher.

Heidi said, "Good, you're just in the nick of time, Dylan." He looked up at us curiously. "This is Mr. and Mrs. Biederman," she said. "The story you wrote is for their book."

We thanked him and leaned down to shake his hand. Then he was out the door just as quickly as he had come in.

Heidi held both hands to her heart as she watched Dylan make his way across the playground. "These children are all so special," she said softly.

Heidi—so are their teachers!

We mentioned to Pam Morrison, Melvin's teacher ("On the Street Where He Lives"), that we planned on having a book-signing in the San Fernando Valley, and we hoped he could be there to sign *his* story. She said, "He's a great kid and I'm sure such an opportunity would mean a lot to him. Just let us know when and where and I'll bring him there myself." We were so impressed that a teacher would drive one of her students fifty miles because she knew he might not have another way of getting there.

As our search continued, the Earth Angels hotline became flooded with calls from all over the United States. One night we even received a call from Santa Claus! Forgetting that we had handed a flyer to one of his elves at a nearby shopping center, we were shocked to hear the voice on the other end of the phone say, "No, this isn't a joke. I'm the Santa from the mall."

He told us he had so many stories of good people that he would have trouble picking just one from his long list. He said he would call back, but he never did. (On Christmas Eve, along with the cookies and milk, we left a pen and paper—just in case.)

While doing the dishes one evening, we listened to the voice mail on our speaker phone. Susan Wright's voice was soft and we had to turn off the water to hear her. "I have an Earth Angel story I would like to tell. It's about my son who died last month."

We looked at each other sadly. She would be our first returned call that evening.

We spoke for nearly two hours about her son, Jason ("Jason, the Invincible"), and a couple of days later, we received a newspaper article from her in the mail. There was a picture of Susan and Jason sitting next to each other, each exhibiting the same bright smile. (Their picture now sits beside the photograph of Ginger and Catherine.) Because of their fight for Jason's lung transplant, thousands of people (possibly millions in years to come) will benefit from their experience. Thank you, Susan, for sharing Jason with all of us.

Although this book is filled with so much light, we were sometimes exposed to a darker side of life. But we were pleasantly surprised to learn that *Earth Angels* often had a positive impact on what seemed like hopeless situations. For example, Marcell Brickey, a junior high school teacher, told us about a student he had not been able to "get through to." It wasn't until he asked his class to write about their Earth Angels that this troubled boy opened up and showed an interest in school. Mr. Brickey told us, "He's been coming to class ever since. You have no idea how much this has affected all of my kids. I plan to make this a classroom assignment every year."

When Dana Karney, the vice principal of Channel Islands High School, called us one afternoon, we realized the impact such an assignment could have. One of the students at Ms. Karney's school revealed, in her story, that she was being abused at home. "She had gone through years of schooling without anyone discovering her terrible situation," Ms. Karney told us. "Because of *Earth Angels*, the young lady is now safe in foster care, and her teacher and I believe this assignment has possibly saved her life."

Little did we know, when we heard about a young girl's life being saved, that we would soon hear about another life that might soon be taken. Byron Ashley Parker, a prisoner on Georgia's death row, sent us a letter. Byron knew his story was, as he put it, "several shades darker than what would be appropriate for this book." Though it was beautifully written, he was right, but through our correspondence with him, we have discovered that even in this darkest of corners, a light can be found. We have kept in touch with Byron, and his picture sits among the other photographs of people who have shown us that goodness can exist anywhere.

When we flip through these pages, we are reminded of the real people who have touched us and have become part of an

Earth Angels family. They are not fictional characters—the people you have met in this book are somewhere in this world. Maybe they are in line next to you at the grocery store or perhaps they live down your street.

These people renewed our faith in human kindness and they inspired us to look for the good in all people. We hope they have had the same effect on you. They also made us aware of the good inside ourselves and of how wonderful it feels to spread it around. All of us have the ability to be Earth Angels. Just think, someday someone might be telling a story about you—*their* Earth Angel.

In some ways *Earth Angels* is a book without an ending. Everyone has a story. Phone calls and letters continue to come in, and we meet people each day who want to share their stories with us, and with you.

Now, do you want to hear the greatest Earth Angel story of them all? Just ask anyone, and they will tell you.

It feels good to experience, acknowledge, and share human kindness. If each of us would just spread our wings—there would be Heaven on Earth.

With love and kindness,
Lorin and Jerry

Live for something—Do good,
and leave behind you a monument of virtue that
the storms of time can never destroy
—Write your name in kindness, love,
and mercy on the hearts of thousands
you come in contact with year by year,
and you will never be forgotten.
Your name and your good deeds will shine
as the stars of heaven.
    —*Chalmers*

Who's Your Earth Angel?
An Invitation to Our Readers

If you have a story about the Earth Angel in *your* life, we'd like to include it in our next book. Please send your story, with a self-addressed stamped envelope, to the following post office box:

EARTH ANGELS
18034 Ventura Boulevard, #414
Encino, California 91316

For more information: E-mail—earthangels@digitalstarlight.com. Web page—www.digitalstarlight.com/earthangels.

Bring the spirit of *Earth Angels* to your school, charitable organization, religious group, or company. Jerry and Lorin Biederman are available to help you implement an Earth Angels Program.

Earth Angels *Staff*

Contributing Writers: Kate Siegel, Carolyn Manea, Greg Asplin, Christopher Owens, Dianne Graf
Assistant Editors: Greg Asplin, Danny Biederman, Jeff Kagan, Deidra Goulding
Public Relations: Samara Iodice, Debbie Cobb
Earth Angels Web Page: Braden Villanueva

Earth Angels Who
Deserve Our Thanks

A special thank you to our Los Angeles literary agent, B. J. Robbins, for giving *Earth Angels* its wings to fly from California to New York (and the world). It was three o'clock in the morning when we finished our proposal for this book and drove to your house to place it on your doorstep. When we awoke, there was a message telling us that you had not only read it over breakfast, but had already begun calling publishers. You are more than we could have asked for in an agent (and a friend). You are *Earth Angels'* Earth Angel.

When B.J. told us what the editor-in-chief of Broadway Books did after reading our proposal, we knew *Earth Angels* had found a home. He shared his very own story at an editorial meeting. Thank you, John Sterling, for your beautiful tribute to the stranger on Occom Pond; the book would not have been complete without it. We are very grateful to our editor, Lauren Marino. We heard you were one of the best in New York—to us, you *are* the best! Thank you, Kati Steele, assistant editor, for putting up with our odd hours, for quickly replying to our barrage of e-mails, and for taking such care of us and this book. It was wonderful to visit the offices of Broadway Books and to meet so many warm, sincere, and talented people. We know each of you are important to *Earth Angels* and we thank you all: William M. Shinker, Maggie Richards, Trigg Robinson, Justin Loeber, Kathy Spinelli, Roberto de Vicq de Cumptich, Rebecca

Holland, Jane Archer, Amy Silveira, and all of you who make Broadway Books so unique and special.

One of the best things about being married to each other is that it has brought together two wonderful families. In our fairy tale, the mothers-in-law are more like fairy godmothers and our brothers and sisters are truly princes and princesses. Thank you for letting us dream our dreams and for helping to make them come true. Carole and Ray Atkinson; Esther and Harry Biederman; Steven Ackrich; Mr. and Mrs. Lee Ackrich; Uncle Sheldon Ackrich; Shae, Raneile, and Milli Atkinson; Danny, Bea, Illya, Moriah, and Bond Biederman; Jay, Debbie, and Allie Bolton; the Breitbarts; Uncle Jules and Aunt Bonnie Bresnick; Chuck, Mila, Inez, and Irene Casper; the Kagans; Dorothy Kaufman and family; the Leifers; the Prices; Elsie Sills; Kathrine Sills; Henny and Gerry "Nana and Papa" Sills; Glen, Jeryl, Tyler, and Carly Uslan; Amy, Sylvia and Irving Wallace; the Wallechinsky family; the Weinroths; and Disney Biederman. We love you all.

A great big hug to our friends, coworkers, and others for your invaluable help with this book and for filling our world with love and laughter: Lisa Alternative; Phyllis Amescua; Patti Breitman; Ray Cázares and Enrique Cázares; Cate Cummings; Lauren Field (BDD); Robert Fields; the Flores family; Bill Goss; Michele Krupp; Robert and Katrina Harp; David Ilan and Aviv Ilan; Angela and Ralph Jimenez; Lisa Jimenez; Kevin and Susan Kinsey; Seung Hee Lee; Roger, Miyoko, and Madison Love and family; Clare Mason; Linnea McCord; Danny McKinley; Pam Morrison; Pamela Nathan; Christopher Owens; Gary and Arleta Owens;

Michael Reiss; Isabel Ramos; Craig and Patti Rosen and family; Daniel Rudy Ruettiger; Dr. Howard Sawyer; Phil Scheinert; Jeanene Shannon; the Sicher family; Tom Silberkleit; Paul Surratt; the Tamburro family; Daniel Taub and Gladys Taub; Dr. Gabriel Tenembaum; Mike Thornton; Jenna Turner; Simone Van Egmond; Kieth Vineyard; Kathy Von Feldt; the Wiener, Solomon, and Stone families; Jackie Wolf; Melvin and Barbara Wolf. The Journalism Department, California State University, Northridge: Dr. Tom Reilly; Henrietta Charles; Elizabeth Whirledge; Maureen Rubin. Great Western Bank: Ed Atkins; Jeff Balaban; Chris Coburn; Lori Depweg; Miguel Fernandez; Michelle Ferrel; Richard Grant; Charles Jones; Lloyd Kaneko; Annette Marufo; Susan Mattison; KC McMinn; Dahlia Mecenas; Byron O'Gilvie; Kelly Raissi; Charyl Sarber; June Yakos. A special thank you to our dear and devoted friend, Andy Shepard, for always being there for us, and for sharing your talents as an editor and publicist.

We would like to acknowledge the following companies—that are not *just* companies, but companies with hearts: Leslie Barton and Maria Bymakos, Leslie Barton Photographer; Promote-It!, InterWeb Connections; Toshiba and Compaq computers; La Fondue Bourguignonne, Sherman Oaks, California; Joseph D. Block and Linelle Springer, law offices of Candiotty and Block; Sonoma County Hilton, Santa Rosa, California; Ron Drake, The Waldorf-Astoria, New York; Scott C. Evans, Omni Berkshire Place, New York; Princeville Hotel, Kauai, Hawaii; ROPA (Regional Organ Procurement Agency); Dalmation Dreams; Book Angels, school library program, Tucson, Arizona; The Walt Disney Company.

Participating Schools and Teachers

Mary Lou Griego, Robertson High School, Las Vegas, New Mexico; Dana Karney, Channel Islands High School, Oxnard, California; Lori Trotter Gully, Riverview High School, Sarasota, Florida; Carol Pim, North Fort Myers High School, Ft. Myers, Florida; Connie Howell, Ontario High School, Ontario, California; John Hynes, Chaminade College Preparatory, West Hills, California; Marcell Brickey, Fremont Intermediate School, Oxnard, California; Dave Baldwin, Ventura High School, Ventura, California; Heidi Detamore, St. Mel School, Woodland Hills, California.

Lorin Michelle Biederman is coauthor of the book *101 Ways to See the Light.* Lorin is also a poet. Her work has been published in several anthologies and has won a number of awards. She has spent several years as a teacher, instructing students on the use of various types of computer software. Lorin has also taught in the corporate arena for such companies as Great Western Bank, Kinko's, Northridge Hospital, Sunkist, and Warner Bros. At present she lives in Woodland Hills, California, with her husband, Jerry, and their dog, Disney.

Jerry Biederman's popular book, *Secrets of a Small Town: The Extraordinary Confessions of Ordinary People*, was the true story of Biederman's journey to a small town "somewhere in America," where he went on "a scavenger hunt" for strangers' secrets. It was a Book-of-the-Month Club alternate selection, was syndicated to more than four hundred newspapers, and was produced as a pilot for a TV series by Twentieth Century-Fox Television.

Jerry coauthored his first book, *The Do-It-Yourself Bestseller*, at the age of twenty-one. It included original story beginnings written by such authors as Stephen King, Barbara Taylor Bradford, Ken Follett, Isaac Asimov, Belva Plain, and Irving Wallace (Jerry's uncle). *The Bestseller* promoted literacy for schoolchildren and was the focus of a national high school writing competition. Another Biederman collection, *My First Real Romance*, was a gathering of true stories about the first real-life romances of twenty bestselling romance writers. This award-winning book reached the Waldenbooks national bestseller list. His book, *He's a Girl!*, was a celebration of "expectant fatherhood." Average fathers at a Los Angeles maternity ward were asked to share their thoughts and feelings on the day of their child's birth. Jerry recently collaborated on *101 Ways to See the Light* with his wife, Lorin. *Earth Angels* is the writing couple's second book collaboration.

Early in his writing career Jerry was dubbed a "West Coast Wunderkind" by *The Washington Post*. He has collaborated on various other literary ventures with authors such as Roald Dahl, Richard Adams, P. L. Travers, Madeleine L'Engle, Rebecca West, and Clare Boothe Luce. Biederman's books have been featured on "Good Morning America" and written about in the *New York Times*, the *Los Angeles Times*, and *People* magazine.